Bing

On the Road to Elko

Bing

On the Road to Elko

Carolyn Schneider

Stephens Press ❧ Las Vegas, Nevada

Editor: Jami Carpenter

Designer: Sue Campbell

Publishing Coodinator: Stacey Fott

Cataloging in Publication

Schneider, Carolyn.

  Bing, on the road to Elko / Carolyn Schneider.

  140 p. : photos ; 23 cm.

ISBN: 1-935043-08-0

ISBN-13: 978-1-935043-08-9

Bing Crosby's niece describes his connections to Nevada when he owned ranches in Elko and his few appearances in Las Vegas.

1. Crosby, Bing, 1903-1977. 2. Elko (Nev.)—History. 3. Singers—United States—Biography. I. Title.

[92] dc22   2009   2009931159

STEPHENS PRESS, LLC
A Stephens Media Company

Post Office Box 1600
Las Vegas, NV 89125-1600

www.stephenspress.com

Printed in Hong Kong

*Dedicated with love to my mother,
Mary Rose Crosby Pool,
because Bing was her hero.*

CONTENTS

Foreword

I WAS HONORED WHEN COUSIN CAROLYN ASKED ME TO WRITE THE foreword for her new book on Uncle Bing's exploits in Nevada ... even more so after I read the manuscript.

The statistics tell the story: Bing Crosby was the most popular entertainer of the last century. He starred in sixty-three feature films, sold over one billion tickets at the box office, recorded over two thousand songs, had thirty-eight No. 1 hits and 368 songs on the charts. These numbers are so far beyond anyone else's that it's like talking about a trillion dollars; the numbers are so big, nobody can even comprehend them!

So what could be left to say? I think you'll find that Carolyn's book on Bing's Nevada days reveals a part of his character that is often missed. Uncle Bing really disliked sycophants, people who would fawn all over him telling him how great he was. He didn't get much of that in Elko. I know he found that very refreshing.

Bing grew up in a working-class Irish American family in Spokane, and he knew about hard work. He worked two and three jobs before and after school as a boy. He not only believed in the value of it, I think he actually liked it! Owning a working ranch in north central Nevada gave him exactly the kind of respite he was seeking, especially during those years when his fame was at its peak.

I think you'll enjoy Carolyn's book about Bing's Nevada days; I know I did. She's got a great title for the book, but I might have suggested an alternative: *Bing Crosby, Regular Guy.*

—*Howard Crosby*
Walla Walla, Washington

Acknowledgments

WHILE I MAY HAVE WRITTEN A GREAT MANY WORDS IN THE PAST FEW years, none of them would ever have been published without the prodding, praise, support, love, and promotion of my husband, Dirk Schneider. It's about time I thank him for everything, so here it is, along with a hug and a kiss.

—Carolyn Schneider

Introduction:
Bing Crosby's Other Life

Most of us are not aware that the history of Nevada includes a long established relationship to Hollywood. The deserts that abound throughout the state have attracted filmmakers since the early 1900s for their beauty and "old West" quality. Even today the television and movie industry looks to locations in Nevada as a backdrop for their stories.

Las Vegas has also become a playground for countless celebrities, and casino showroom headliners were well-known names in the entertainment business. These performers were not movie stars per se, but singers, dancers, and musicians.

A number of film stars from the 1930s and '40s visited Nevada, and some even bought homes there, but none of them ever became a "true Nevadan" by local standards, except Bing Crosby, who purchased large cattle ranches in the northern part of the state, near Elko. Bing's acceptance by the residents was probably because of his casual attitude towards his own celebrity status and willingness to "fit in" with his surroundings. Uncle Bing was captivated by the land and people of Nevada. He was once quoted as saying "I'm in love with these folks," and that affection was returned many times over the years.

It is believed that Bing first encountered Elko County when he was returning from a hunting trip to Canada and Idaho. The highway leading south into Nevada takes the traveler directly into the heart of Elko, a city of about five thousand people at that time, around 1942.

Uncle Bing was an avid golfer, fisherman, hunter, and all around outdoorsman. Living and working in Hollywood satisfied his passion for golf, but not his other interests. Whenever he was able to spend time in Nevada, it was the best of all worlds for him. I don't believe Uncle Bing spent much, if any, time in Reno, but Las Vegas and Elko played host to him and his family frequently during a fifteen-year period.

Bing's Elko properties provided him with the outdoor ranch life that he grew to love, as well as excellent fishing and hunting grounds. He introduced his four young sons to that lifestyle when he bought his first cattle ranch not far from Elko in 1943. Some years later, my mother and I visited the ranches that Uncle Bing enjoyed so much.

The first recorded visit of my uncle to Las Vegas was in 1956. It was golf that lured him and brought him back a number of times. He also made several trips to Las Vegas to be in the audience and show support for the young members of the Crosby clan who were performing on stage there.

Although Bing was never booked to perform into any of the Vegas hotel-casinos, he did appear one time (for a one-night concert) at the Aladdin Theatre for the Performing Arts. This was a fund-raising event organized by a local priest who had virtually no assets. The priest was under orders, however, to build a church in a particular section of Las Vegas. Uncle Bing's concert raised the money to get the project started and the following year it was completed. I visited that church thirty years later, and met with the priest, the first Crosby family member to do so.

I think the life and times of Bing Crosby in Nevada gives us an insight into the man that, until now, has not been widely publicized. Let us begin.

Prologue:
Finding Elko

WELCOME TO THE WORLD OF ELKO, NEVADA. IF YOU LIKE OLD MOVIES, charge accounts, and *Mayberry RFD*, you're gonna love this town. It's a place where the cattle are fat, the women are faithful, and a man's word is his bond. Business deals are sealed with a handshake, and if a man is called a "straight shooter," it usually means he only throws the bull around at the yearly rodeo. Uncle Bing called it "one of the last bastions of the Old West," but you might just call it old fashioned.

Elko was a big money town, because of cattle and land transactions that were done without any cut-throat tactics like the big cities. Cattle men are known to be very fair when it comes to making business deals. Up around Elko, the buying and selling of ranch land or cattle is easily done by a couple of fellas leaning on a fence in the corral.

Elko, population fifteen thousand, is the namesake of Elko County, a vast expanse of land in Northern Nevada. Approximately seventeen hundred square miles, it is the heart of cattle country and probably considered the livestock capital between the Rocky Mountains and the Pacific Ocean. Picturesque and bucolic by any standards, Elko and the surrounding areas attract outdoor enthusiasts year 'round for the hunting, fishing, and hiking opportunities as well as the scenic views. The rugged Ruby Mountains, sometimes called "the Alps of Nevada," lie twenty-one miles to the southeast of Elko and provide a welcome, cool retreat during the hot summer months.

Situated on the main east-west interstate highway 80, Elko is approximately halfway between Reno and Salt Lake City. To the south, it is a six-hour drive to Las Vegas. Although it's not a metropolis, many travelers have stopped and spent time in Elko ever since the hotels were built there. In spite of its location, this town with a heavy western accent continues to offer both locals and visitors some of the best activities and entertainment available. Beginning with Newt Crumley's hotel in 1941 and followed by others, the lounges and showrooms of the various establishments boasted of appearances by some of the top flight performances of the day. Half–page ads in the *Elko Independent* and later the *Daily Free Press* showed photos of well-known, recognizable singers, bands, and musicians. If you are of the age to remember those days, you will surely recall: Sophie Tucker, Sons of the Pioneers, Ted Lewis, and the Paul Whitman orchestra, to name but a few. All of these acts took to the stage under the spotlights at establishments such as: the Commercial Hotel, Ranchinn, and Stockmen's Hotel.

When Uncle Bing was around Elko in the '40s he performed a few times, but not for money. It was either for a fundraiser or as a favor for his friend, hotelier Newt Crumley. The Commercial had a nice-sized bandstand and stage for performances. But it wasn't until about 1959 that Mr. Crumley had to call in construction workers to knock out part of the back wall to create a stage door entrance. The reason: to accommodate his new underage singing sensation, Wayne Newton. According to Nevada law at that time, a teenager was not allowed to walk through a casino to get onto the stage. Newton was twelve years old when he started performing in Elko.

The town had a reputation for friendliness, combined with a down home attitude. These qualities, along with a wide choice of entertainment, the prospect of ranch life, and an atmosphere of safety were some of the characteristics that prompted Uncle Bing to remark, "this is a great place to raise kids."

Chapter One: Makin' Whoopee

To understand my uncle's love for the town of Elko, in northeastern Nevada, you must start in Las Vegas. Not only because it's an absolutely fabulous city, but also because my uncle Bing visited there many times and really enjoyed it.

Known around the world as a sort of Disneyland for adults, Las Vegas also has some of the finest restaurants and best entertainment to be found anywhere, and though gaming is the main attraction, I don't think Uncle Bing was part of the casino scene. Somehow I can't envision him pulling the handle on those old time one-arm-bandits, or spreading himself across the end of one of those large tables to throw dice and engage in a game called "craps." No, no, not Uncle Bing. Except for horse racing, which he looked upon as "the sport of kings," the appeal for him, naturally, were the numerous lush golf courses and the year-round sunny days.

There were a few Hollywood stars who really did get into the action on the green felt gaming tables of Vegas. Some of them lost huge amounts of money, while others were such big winners that the hotels wined and dined them, provided a chauffeured limousine, and the most elaborate suite of rooms available.

Others, like Dean Martin and Sammy Davis Jr. would go into the casinos after their performance in the showroom and join the crowds playing craps or blackjack. Usually this would wind up being an absolute laugh riot as Sammy and Dean took turns acting as the card dealer or throwing the dice up in the air at the crap table. It was all in good fun, the people loved it, management allowed it, and a lot of good publicity was gained from it.

Bing, however, was not a man who spent his money on a whim; that's not what his book *Call Me Lucky* is about. He had investments, to be sure, as well as owning businesses and property. But those things were not considered gambles; they were regarded as part of financial planning, orchestrated by Bing's brother, Everett, and were done in the privacy of his office.

Those were the days — in the 1950s — when Americans frequently consulted with AAA for travel plans and maps that would take them to Las Vegas. The public demand for more and more hotel rooms led to a building boom, with each hotel vying for tourist business. It became a competition to see which hotel-casino would be the biggest, the most dazzling, and the most exciting.

About this time, the casino bosses and owners began to realize that the fun-seekers who came to Vegas were looking for an alternative pastime to gaming. Several hotels were now classified as resorts, and along with that came the demand for even more diverse entertainment. After all, they rationalized, they already had slot machines and roulette; it was time to add some new and unique feature to their hotels to draw players to their casinos and keep them spending money. Thus the "headliner" system was born on the Las Vegas "Strip." Big name stars like Liberace and Frank Sinatra increased the wattage on the enormous neon signs that graced the entrances of the major hotels such as Caesars Palace, the Sands, Tropicana, and the Dunes.

One of these, the Desert Inn, was the only Las Vegas Strip hotel to boast having a golf course. Owner Wilber Clark was well aware of the advantage, offering guests a complete entertainment package, which included eighteen holes of golf. It became so popular that in 1952, Clark initiated the Tournament of Champions, thereby putting the public image of his hotel at better than par. It was this tournament and the guest line-up of celebrity golfers that attracted Uncle Bing to take part in the event in 1956. Along with his pals Bob Hope and Phil Harris, Bing was a welcome participant and was interviewed by local radio station KENO. Prior to teeing off for the first round, Bing met with TV star Desi Arnaz, and the two amateur golfers helped plan this Pro-Am, which was nationally televised. Phil Harris had agreed to provide some colorful commentary during the match, as only he could do.

The crowd in the gallery voiced their approval as Bing and comic Ben Blue appeared on the links. Although it was April, the desert air held a slight chill, enough for Bing to button up his light-colored golfing sweater with the full sleeves and tightly-knit cuffs. Never a fashion plate, Uncle Bing wore his tweedy-looking trousers with pleated fronts and an open collar sport shirt. Completing his ensemble was the ever-present golf cap, the one I didn't care much for because it made his ears stick out more than usual.

The following year Bing again signed on to play in what was becoming a Desert Inn classic, the Tournament of Champions. This time he arrived at the airport (which back then was called McCarran Field), with son Dennis, professional golfer Jimmy Demaret, and Bing's sidekick, Phil Harris. The tournament was scheduled to begin on Thursday, but the players always arrived a few days early, in order to get in some practice rounds and get a feel for the course. As a warm-up for themselves and the gathering crowd, Bing and popular newscaster Walter Winchell held a putting contest. I don't recall who won; I'm still in shock to learn that Walter even played golf! In the amateur pairings of 1957, Hope and Harris defeated Crosby and Winchell.

It wasn't until 1959 that Uncle Bing appeared again at the Desert Inn Country Club to play with Hope and Harris in the Tournament of Champions.

In the interim, he returned to Las Vegas a number of times, most notably in 1957 to remarry, having lost his first wife, Dixie Lee, to cancer in 1952.

Bing's career was anchored in Los Angeles and Hollywood, although he did a great deal of traveling for both business and pleasure here and abroad. He was not a household name around Las Vegas the way Elvis, Sinatra, and others had become, yet as a world-renowned performer, and by this time a Nevada rancher, he received an honor of sorts.

❦

Bing was very much part of the Desert Inn Tournament of Champions.

Bob Hope, Phil Harris, and Bing check the golf line-up for the tournament at Desert Inn.

Who says you can't distract a golfer?

From left to right: Phil Harris, Walter Winchell, Bing, and Bob Hope.

*How many Marx Brothers can fit on a golf cart? Add Bing,
Dean Martin, and a couple of cuties and you have the answer.*

*Bing and his second wife,
Kathryn, depart for their
honeymoon after being
married in Las Vegas.*

Chapter One: *Makin' Whoopee*

The Sands of Time

THE SANDS HOTEL WAS ONE OF THE NEWER AND VERY POPULAR GATH-ering places on the Strip for the "in" crowd. To commemorate its first full year in operation, hotel executive Jack Entratter ordered a time capsule to be planted into the ground on the Sands property. It was in 1953, and the items chosen to be placed inside the twelve-foot aluminum capsule, shaped like a rocket, were meant to give future generations a sample of meaningful memorabilia of the era. Included were: Bing's pipe, the boxing gloves worn by Sugar Ray Robinson when he won the middleweight crown, a pair of Ray Bolger's dancing shoes, and a wax impression of Jimmy Durante's nose.

The capsule was forgotten over the next two decades, but was discovered in the late 1970s when construction work began in order to expand the hotel property. New items of interest were added and the capsule was replanted.

The infamous time capsule of 1953 and 1978 lay buried for another twenty years until the Sands Hotel property was sold and the buildings were imploded. Once again, construction equipment was brought to the site, making way for the elegant Venetian Hotel and Casino. Just as before, the capsule was unearthed, but not reburied. This time the owners of the proposed new hotel had the capsule taken to their home and opened the hatch. Unfortunately, the aluminum shell had been pierced over the years and water had leaked inside; much of the contents were unrecognizable, and rotted away into slush. The stacks of newspapers had to be thrown away, as well as any fabric that had not been properly wrapped and sealed. Surprising, though, some of the memorabilia was unscathed: a suit that had belonged to Frank Sinatra, jewelry and a suit from Sammy Davis Jr., a pair of shoes, and other miscellaneous items. The importance of the "Rat Pack" was duly noted and seemed to be the things of greatest value. Sorry, no sign of Bing's pipe.

Bing's son Gary was also gaining popularity during these years, having been featured on the front cover of *Life* magazine's July 30, 1951 issue.

Tallulah Bankhead helped the Sands Hotel celebrate its first
year in 1953 with sinking of a time capsule. Memorabilia
included Bing Crosby's pipe, Sugar Ray Robinson's boxing
gloves, and Ray Bolger's dancing shoes.

Chapter One: *Makin' Whoopee*

By the summer of 1959, Bing's four sons had formed a singing act and performed as "The Crosby Boys," debuting at the Sky Room in Tucson, Arizona. They also appeared at the Moulin Rouge in Hollywood. The plan was to try the act on an out-of-town audience, with the ultimate goal of being booked into Las Vegas.

The show went well and they were sold out most nights, though there was tension among the brothers. After some heated discussions, Gary left the act and went out on his own. He showcased his talent as a single performer in Las Vegas in 1960; his three brothers appeared there a year later.

I was invited to attend the performance when my cousin Gary appeared on stage at the Flamingo Hotel in Las Vegas in August of 1960. His dear old dad was right there to give him moral support. "Bing Joins Gary on Vegas Stage" said the headline of the local paper, along with a photo and caption that read: "Crosby Duet." Because Uncle Bing had never stepped onto a stage in Las Vegas before, this seems to have cre-

ated big news. That night Gary had gone through his regular routine of mimicking his father when he took the microphone, and introduced him by saying, "there's a man in the audience who taught me all of this." It caught the Flamingo showroom crowd completely by surprise.

Bing rose from his seat and walked toward the front of the room. After climbing a few steps, he strolled onto the stage. He stood next to Gary, sharing the one and only microphone, and appeared

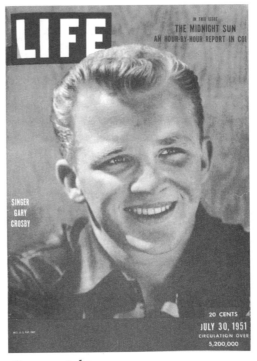

Gary at eighteen.

more casual than usual. Without his toupee that evening, few people sitting near him in the audience recognized the crooner until he was under the spotlights. Although it was the peak of the summer heat in Las Vegas, back in the 1960s the better restaurants and showrooms had a dress code that required men to wear a jacket. Even someone as well-known as Bing would not have been admitted if he arrived in one of his famous Hawaiian shirts. Thanks to air conditioning, Gary's dad looked very sharp indeed wearing a linen sport coat and tan trousers.

The two men started off with some light-hearted banter and a bit of clowning around. Assuming that was to be the end of it, Uncle Bing started to exit the stage, not wanting to steal Gary's big moment. Besides, Bing had never worked a Vegas nightclub crowd before and wasn't at all sure what to expect and he had made some noise about not wanting to perform in Las Vegas when he was interviewed some time before. So now he was caught in the crosshairs, feeling a bit unsure of the situation, when Gary tugged on his arm and asked him to "stick around." Bing stood there with his hands in his pockets, looking like someone who had just been pulled out of the audience by a magician to take part in a knife-throwing act. But the old master quickly recovered and joined Gary in a duet of their popular recording, "A Simple Melody." Bing was in good sprits and the father-son team did some additional ad-libbing on stage; the people loved it. "I'm glad to see you're finally working," Bing said to his oldest son. It was a packed house for the dinner show that night, and even Uncle Bing's pal Phil Harris was sitting ringside.

In 1961, the three Crosby brothers appeared in Las Vegas at the Desert Inn, one of their father's favorite spots for golf and relaxation. No one had to twist Bing's arm to spend a couple of days in Vegas and catch the boys' act in the Painted Desert Room of the resort hotel. Booked for a four-week stint, the brothers — Phil, Dennis, and Lindsay — shared the stage with comic Dick Shawn, creating an evening of music and light-hearted repartee. A local orchestra and a chorus of dancers rounded out the bill. The show opened on Tuesday night, thereby giving locals the first chance at tickets for the performance. Coincidentally, the Crosbys and Shawn had worked together in Frank Sinatra's film, *Soldiers 3*, fea-

Chapter One: *Makin' Whoopee*

Gary gets a few performance tips from dear old dad in his dressing room.

These three aces could have been four of a kind if Gary had stayed with the act.

turing the famous Rat Pack of Sinatra, Dean Martin, and Sammy Davis Jr., plus Peter Lawford and Joey Bishop.

The Crosby trio staged an entirely new act, one without Gary, which was put together for them by some of Hollywood's top nightclub producers. The sons of Bing Crosby never had trouble finding willing helpers. The first of two medleys the boys performed included some folk songs they remembered from childhood, sung to them, of course, by the world's greatest crooner. Also on the program was a medley of about thirty songs made famous by their father during his career thus far; this made a very fine tribute to Bing and was actually the high point of the act. Interviewed backstage afterward, Bing was asked his opinion of the show. "I thought the boys mixed it up pretty good," he said.

Bing stayed on in Las Vegas for a few days at the Desert Inn to play golf.

Las Vegas saw more of the Crosbys in the ensuing years. Gary, seeking an acting career as well as singing, was booked into Caesars Palace in August of 1967 as a cast member of *The Odd Couple*, a stage presentation, something new on the Las Vegas strip. The leading roles were played by Tony Randall and Mickey Rooney. Also appearing as their poker buddies were Arnold Stang, Buddy Lester, Sugar Ray Robinson, and Gary.

In 1970, Gary was at the Sands Hotel in Las Vegas for a part in the television series, *Julia*, starring Diahann Carroll which was being filmed there.

The prelude to all of this interest and activity in Las Vegas was Bing's arrival in Nevada via Elko. While the amenities offered by Vegas appealed to the showman in Uncle Bing, it was the total absence of show business that called to him from the land of northeastern Nevada. On the many occasions when he wanted to truly get away and relax, he would pack his boots and Levis and head for cattle country.

Chapter Two:
Home on the Range

BING'S FONDNESS FOR HORSES AND RACING WERE WELL KNOWN back in 1936 when he built the Del Mar racetrack in California. It was also the year he starred in the film *Rhythm on the Range*; he played the part of a singing cowboy and said it was one of his favorite roles. The movie posters promoting the picture show Bing in a satin western shirt and neckerchief.

Some people feel that by working on the film, which was shot on location in the High Sierra mountains, Bing got a taste of ranch life that whetted his appetite to make it a reality. It would be quite a few years, however, before Uncle Bing bought his first ranch; not in California, but in northeastern Nevada, near Elko.

Listed for sale as the "7 Js Livestock Co.," the property was also known as the Jube Wright Ranch. In any case, Uncle Bing literally took the bull by the horns and entered into the world of ranch ownership and raising cattle.

As many of us are prone to do, Bing made the mistake of buying property that he knew little about. It was so close to the Humboldt River that when the river overflowed its banks the year after he bought it, Bing's land was flooded.

Enter John Oldham, a real estate broker who dealt primarily with ranch properties. He became a very close friend of Uncle Bing's; the two men formed a bond of friendship through both business dealings and love of the outdoors. John was quite a hunter and an excellent shot, and he joined Bing frequently over the years to hunt game.

After the flood, Bing called John to inquire about another ranch, the Quarter Circle S near Tuscarora that he heard was for sale. Apparently Bing thought moving to a spread further up north would avoid future problems like flooding.

This was a big step, even a risk for my uncle, because of the size of the operation and the complete change of lifestyle it would require for his entire family. Could he handle a property of this size? Would his wife Dixie and the boys like it up there? The first ranch that he purchased wasn't too far from civilization, but this one was more isolated. I know that Uncle Bing wanted to teach his sons the facts of real life, not the phony, make-believe world of the movie business. But Aunt Dixie was another matter; she was a "city girl" and not accustomed to being without her card-playing friends.

Nevertheless, in 1944, Bing told John Oldham to go ahead and make the deal to buy the property with its cow-calf operation.

The Quarter Circle S Ranch

A LONG WAY FROM THE FAST-PACED AND CELEBRITY LIFESTYLE OF Hollywood is the Quarter Circle S Ranch. You would hardly recognize the famous singer if you were to see him at his ranch. Dressed in working clothes, Bing fooled anyone who showed up unexpectedly asking directions to the Crosby ranch. His jeans sported a hole or two and his cowboy hat looked as though his horse had stepped on it.

Yet this was the man who owned and operated an eighty-seven hundred acre spread, located about eight hundred miles from his home in the film capital. He spent most of every summer in the northern part of Nevada overseeing and working on one of seven ranches he owned. Bing was a genuine rancher and the properties he purchased were cattle operations that ran full time. The twenty-six hundred head of Hereford, counted at the last round-up, is testament to the fact that Uncle Bing was serious about having money-making enterprises, as well as a getaway place for the present and future.

This location also had a stable full of horses, used for the Binglin Stock Farm, an enterprise Bing shared with his friend Lindsay Howard. The purpose was to provide breeding and racing stock for tracks throughout

Above: Movie poster from 1936. Below: Uncle Bing is dressed the part for
Rhythm on the Range. *A number of years later he would be in Western
garb every day in the summer, working on his ranches near Elko.*

the west. The Howard family was well-known in racing circles, having once owned the famous Seabiscuit.

Mother and I visited there at the request of Uncle Bing, curious to see the old cowhand in action. As I recall, finding this ranch was tricky for anyone not familiar driving the area outside of Elko. By their very nature, ranches are not located along major highways; visitors wanting to locate the Circle S should get directions to the town nearest the ranch, which is Tuscarora. After turning off from the main road, it was another four miles along a route that was badly rutted from the weather and cattle trucks. Still, the drive was pleasant. Cattle roamed over the vast valley of the ranch, surrounded by mountains, creating a very bucolic scene. A mining town in the past, it was once inhabited by five thousand Chinese who worked in the mines.

The ranch house itself was enclosed by a classic white picket fence, and the single story structure was painted brown. The interior was all knotty pine and had three bedrooms and two baths. Built as a no-frills residence for cowboys before Uncle Bing bought it, the house had no living room or fireplace; he added those amenities before he moved in.

Life on a cattle ranch is not for slackers; everyone works and pulls their own weight, even the boss. The day began at 5:30 a.m. when seventy-two-year-old Chinese Charlie rang the breakfast bell, and you had better heed the call or you'd miss out on the meal because as Charlie told me, he didn't give room service. Far from being a gourmet chef, he was a good cook who just made down-home meals. The ranch hands said that when Charlie made soup it was thick enough to walk on.

We were a couple of greenhorns when it came to cowboy cuisine. For one thing, we were not accustomed to having a big meal at noon. Secondly, when Charlie brought out our first breakfast of mush, sausage, bacon, eggs, and deer liver, we felt guilty for not loading our plates. I began to think that we probably should have stayed in town at a hotel, because we felt a little out of place. But Mother was a trooper and as long as she could maintain her tradition of having an evening cocktail, she was fine.

After breakfast that first day, Uncle Bing got up from the table and went over to the lighted gun cabinet across the room to check on his hunting rifles. When his dog Bullet saw him take out one of the guns, he sat at Bing's feet wagging his tail in anticipation of going on a shoot. There were about a dozen rifles in the cabinet and Bing had picked out his favorite, the one he called "Mr. Lucky."

The Circle S had an abundance of deer and wild game, and two wonderful trout streams. Uncle Bing had a number of men friends in Hollywood who also enjoyed ranch life, hunting, and fishing. Clark Gable and Gary Cooper are two that I'm aware of who accepted invitations to come and throw a line in the stream, or use a couple of those guns in the cabinet. They enjoyed Bing's hideaway as much as he did.

It was a regular morning ritual, Mother and I learned, for my uncle to go riding for an hour or so. He told us he found it very relaxing to get out on the ranch for an early morning ride with just his dogs and his horse. We watched him from the window as he placed the bit in the mouth of his horse, Doc, followed by a Mexican saddle blanket and his light brown western saddle. Taking one last tug on the saddle's cinch, he grabbed the reins and took them to the saddle horn. Then his left boot went in the stirrup, his other leg pushed him up and onto the saddle; he was astride the horse in one smooth motion. It was a memorable sight, the singing cowboy with his horse and a dog named Bullet.

Uncle Bing stayed there with us for a few days, and then went over to the PX Ranch to check on things with his ranch foreman, Johnny Eacret.

The Spring Creek Ranch

THE THIRD NEVADA RANCH THAT UNCLE BING PURCHASED WAS Spring Creek, in 1947. It was the largest of his holdings so far, twenty-five thousand acres, and ran three thousand head of white-faced Herefords. It also was an up-and-running operation when Bing contacted his broker, John Oldham, to make arrangements to buy the property. Uncle Bing kept calling it "El Rancho Grande."

Located sixty miles north of Elko, the ranch was in the heart of the Nevada cow country that Bing so dearly loved. He bought the Spring Creek, along with all the other ranches, in the hope that one or more of his four sons would pursue the life their father had started there.

Yet that was not to be the case.

Pheasant anyone?

The advantage of owning your own ranch.

Gary, the oldest boy, lost interest when he graduated from high school. Bing's twins, Phillip and Dennis, tried a short stint at Washington State College to study ranch management and animal husbandry, but to no avail. It has been said by the local people that Bing brought his boys up to Elko too late, that they were too old to embrace ranching as a life career.

While they were still in their early teenage years, however, and as soon as school was out for the summer months, Bing and Dixie would pack up their four sons and head for Nevada and the Spring Creek Ranch. Other Hollywood offspring may have led gilded lives, but not this quartet. Dixie was in agreement with her husband that the Crosby boys were not going to become spoiled brats, products of indulgent parents, which was all too common in the entertainment industry. Instead, the boys were to work as ranch hands, receiving the same pay, and doing the same work as the other men. Some days they might be tending to the horses or helping to brand cattle. In the middle of summer it was time for haying and the boys each handled a pitchfork like seasoned ranch hands. Those months spent at this ranch, or one of the others that Bing owned, were meant to be a character-building experience for the boys. Bing and Dixie wanted to teach their sons the value of hard work as well as the "value of a buck," Aunt Dixie said.

Without a doubt, mealtimes on a ranch were as popular as chewing tobacco and just about as satisfying. Right outside the door of the cookhouse was a large brass bell mounted on a twelve-foot pole. The rope tied to the ringing arm hung within easy reach of anyone doing the cooking and ready to serve the meal. Fresh air and hard work made men hungry, and a single clap of the bell was usually all it took to bring them to the table. During peak times the Spring Creek employed fifty to sixty eager ranch hands. The biggest meal of the day was at noon, or actually about 11:30 a.m., with plenty of food and not much in the way of ambiance. No doilies or flowers on the table the way Aunt Dixie was accustomed to back home, but she was a good sport about being a rancher's wife and played the role to quiet applause.

Uncle Bing seemed to enjoy every one of his cattle-ranching properties; each had its own appeal, he told my mother. At the Spring Creek, it was the vast wilderness area that allowed him to hunt deer and pheasant that he liked about the place. But most of all, it was the chance to do some fishing any time he felt like it. Bing had bought this ranch as an investment and it proved to be a good decision. After buying two more ranches in the vicinity, he built a reservoir that was said to be the finest in Elko County and thus provided Uncle Bing with sport, in addition to the water. He loved the mountain trout he caught there and could be seen on any given day wearing his waders and standing waist deep in the water, baiting his hook and smoking his pipe. Folks in the area claimed they could hear him whistling or humming a tune while he fished, probably something like "Gone Fishin" or "Small Fry," I suppose. Up there he even passed up playing golf to go fishing.

While each of my uncle's ranches had some similarities, there were differences also. At Spring Creek, for instance, there was a main house of seven rooms, with bunk houses across the road. Everyone went to the cookhouse for meals, including the ranch foreman and his wife.

There was a fully stocked machine shop that could handle almost any equipment repair. The Crosby boys were learning the many facets of running a cattle ranch, and learning how to deal with the hay baler or tractor was part of it. More than once Gary had stripped the gears on the Caterpillar diesel tractor.

It was easy to spot the large barn with a "Positively No Smoking" sign over the door. Also, an outstanding feature at this ranch was the totem pole given to Uncle Bing which was erected in the yard near the bunkhouses.

Bing's favorite breed of dog was the Labrador retriever; he owned several of them that he used for hunting birds, such as pheasant or duck. There were usually a few black Labs lazing around on the ranch, but as soon as Bing would reach for one of his rifles, the dogs wagged their tails furiously, letting Bing know they were ready to go.

By 1950, Uncle Bing had put many an hour in the saddle and was now well-versed in the knowledge of horses, cattle, and the rugged life on a Nevada ranch. So he was wise enough to realize that when he got up to those famous ears of his with career demands, it was time to go to Elko and relax. Such was the case that at the completion of filming *Here Comes the Groom*, Bing took a month off to spend at the Spring Creek

Ranch. Once he got there, it was always the same; he would saddle-up Thunder and go ride the range.

Love Thy Neighbor

FOR ALL OF THE QUALITIES ATTRIBUTED TO UNCLE BING, I THINK QUIet generosity was one of his finest. He had been known to help his fellow ranchers, even his own ranch hands.

One such documented incident involved Jess and Louise Botsford who worked for Bing and lived on his Spring Creek Ranch. Jess suffered a heart attack and was taken to the hospital in Elko. Bing expressed great concern regarding the man's condition, and although Jess would not be able to return to work for quite a while, Bing kept him on the payroll at the ranch. In addition, Uncle Bing paid off all the medical bills for Jess and even picked up the tab for a few trips to California that he and Louise made in order to see a specialist after being released from the hospital. The Botsfords stayed in a hotel for a few days while Jess was being examined and treated, and Bing sent flowers to their room during their stay. These acts of kindness show that their relationship was more than just as employer and employee; it's what friends do to help each other.

The PX Ranch

BY THE TIME UNCLE BING COMPLETED HIS PLANS OF OWNING PROPERties in Elko County, his ranch holdings were of tremendous size.

The equipment needed to run an operation this big was an investment in itself. Fourteen tractors worked the Crosby ranch, plus trucks, smaller equipment, and countless items in the tool shed. No wonder they needed a full time grease monkey.

Because Bing had his own hydro-electric plant for light and power on his spread, it helped prevent problems in bad weather. That, along with the cost advantage, proved to be an important asset.

It's been said that a person could ride the range of Uncle Bing's ranch for days without seeing any sign of human habitation. Yet at the same time, in 1951, Bing put in an airstrip large enough for a twin-engine plane to land to accommodate his visitors from California who were anxious to join him for a free and easy getaway.

In the summer months, the cattle roamed Bing's thousands of acres of grazing land. At the same time, thirty-five ranch hands, including the four Crosby boys, were cutting and stacking hay to feed the herd in the winter. It took sixty days of working the hay to supply the hungry Herefords once winter began.

The ranch belonging to Uncle Bing that I visited the most, and remember best, is still called "the PX." It was considered a sort of "home base" by my uncle and the family and was the place Aunt Dixie preferred to stay when she and Bing went up to Elko. It was located sixty-seven miles north of town and I recall what a long and boring drive it was making the trip as a fourteen-year-old girl with my mother. Not much to look at in the way of scenery, only a couple of houses in all those miles, but plenty of jack rabbits. When you're in cow-country like this, the traveling time, or distance, is not considered important.

The PX was a combination of the seven ranches that Uncle Bing owned and operated in northern Nevada. His love of outdoor sports and ranch life prompted him to invest his time and money in these cattle-raising properties. Back in Las Angeles, I don't think Bing's brother, Everett, thought much of the proposition. As Bing's business manager and agent, however, I imagine he pretty much let him have whatever he wanted, provided the risk was not too great. Bing's movie at this time, *Riding High,* seemed to be a case of life imitating art. Not only was he considered a world class entertainer, but he was also becoming a cattle rancher with impressive land holdings. His reputation as a working rancher rather than "just some rich city slicker" gave him a home run with the local fans.

To the best of my knowledge, my mother was the only one of Bing's siblings to ever visit any of his ranches; she was interested in everything Bing did and wanted to be a part of his life whenever possible. So it was no surprise when she told me we were going to visit the PX. When we arrived the noonday meal was being served; the tables were covered with red-and-white-checkered picnic cloths. Jars of mustard, bottles of ketchup, and steak sauce were planted in the center within easy reach of all the ranch hands.

Above: Bing shows off his hunting skills.
Below: Bing with Newt Crumley, plus a couple of pals,
roughing it while hunting.

Uncle Bing sat at the head of the main table and greeted us as we came into the cookhouse. He gave Mother and me a welcoming hug. His boys, my four cousins, just said "hello," skipping the formalities in favor of tying on the old feed bag. "Sit yourselves down and dig in," he said. The food was served family style, with huge platters of roast beef and pork chops being passed around for each person to help themselves. Next came large bowls of mashed potatoes with plenty of gravy, ears of corn, big pitchers of milk, bread, butter, and jam. Fresh homemade berry pie was the finishing touch. Because Bing's Elko neighbors knew him as a working rancher, not a big celebrity, he was able to lead an ordinary life here, and anyone who worked for him on the PX gave him high marks as a boss. From the ranch hands to the cook, to the cowboys and wranglers, everyone knew that Bing wanted to be very much a part of this working cattle ranch. He saddled his own horse and rubbed it down after a ride. This was not a showplace, and there was no conversation about movies or radio or gold records. Uncle Bing looked every bit the part, too, sitting there in a short sleeve western shirt with pearl buttons, his cowboy hat hanging on a wall peg.

Once their plates were cleaned and their belts let out a notch, the boys told Mother and me, or anyone else who asked, that they really liked working on the ranch. Even though it was hard physical labor, "it's better than school," they said. The boys worked together as a team with the other ranch hands, except Lindsay, the youngest. "He gets all the soft jobs," according to the other boys. To hear them tell it, Lindsay just sat around all day and didn't even get his boots dirty. Actually, he did chores around the house and helped the cook, because Uncle Bing didn't want him to wander off very far.

This ranch is where I first met Doris and John Eacret. As ranch foreman, Johnny handled all aspects of the cow-calf operation there and regularly kept in touch with Bing. His wife, Doris, was an accomplished pilot and Johnny was proud to tell folks that she had raced in the Powder Puff Derby. Her flying skills came in handy whenever other ranchers like Newt Crumley needed an overhead view of their vast ranch holdings.

The main house was an unpretentious bungalow with bedrooms, a den, living room, dining room, and kitchen. Doris helped Mother and

Above: Picture of a hardworking rancher.
Below: A day "off," time for clean clothes.

Phil learns to drive.

Above: Gary learns to ride. Above right: It must be Minute Maid. Below left: A call to dinner. Below right: A genuine rancher saddles his own horse.

me get settled in, and then gave us a brief tour of the place. Five small cabins were near the house, the living quarters for the hired hands.

The PX is where Uncle Bing took care of business and would dictate letters to be sent to his office in Hollywood. Ranch business was conducted there also, and Johnny would stop by to go over future plans for the ranch. The PX is also where I met TJ, my riding mentor.

Ragtime Cowboy Joe

HE WAS DESCRIBED AS BEING "CRUSTY," BUT ACTUALLY AN "OLD SALT" would have been more accurate and suited him better. TJ spent his youth at sea, having lied about his age to join the Navy at fifteen. Everyone in the small Idaho community where he was born and raised knew him to be a good boy and a big help to his father on their hundred acres of land. It was partially a farm, growing a few row crops, but mostly potatoes, with the balance of the property being set aside for raising cattle.

So it came as a surprise to most of the people who greeted his family after church that Sunday to learn that TJ had left the land in favor of the sea. It seemed so out of place, a farm boy on the ocean someplace; he probably didn't even know how to swim. What on earth would make him want to do such a thing, they wondered. Little did TJ, or anyone else for that matter, ever imagine what the world would be facing in the ten years ahead. When his twenty-fifth birthday came around, TJ had fully grown into manhood. His travels in the Navy had given this once simple boy without much education a doctorate degree on the subject of life. Now complete with a tattoo on each arm, these blue-ink diplomas of his were like a badge of service to everyone he met and TJ was proud to show them off. The tattoos were testament to the years he spent in foreign lands, places that were totally unknown to the folks back home in Idaho.

He lived through some harrowing times, but returned unscathed to visit the home place from time to time, whenever the Navy allowed him shore leave. He thought about going back into ranching when his time was up with the service, and even married a girl he met at a pot luck supper at the Grange Hall. But the marriage didn't last. TJ was not the kind of man to settle down, much less raise a family; he had lived independently for too long, and was a stranger to responsibility.

When he finally decided, after many years of service, to commit to life on terra firma rather than on a ship, he was sixty-five years old. Now out of the Navy and out of a job, TJ went looking for a quiet place to spend balance of his life.

The idea of farming life again was not as appealing as working with horses and cattle, and the best place to look for work as a wrangler was northern Nevada, just over the Idaho boarder. When TJ hit the road in his Chevy pick-up with the primer gray fender, the day was bright and clear. He took this as an omen to his future that lay ahead.

After stopping for gas, a thermos of hot coffee, and a visit to the room marked "Cowboys," TJ set off for Elko. He figured that would be the best place to go and ask around town about ranching jobs. The feed stores or the local bar were places where cowpokes could usually be found, and were known to be a good source of ranch gossip. Arriving before dark, TJ had a chance to make some inquiries, and got a couple of solid leads for employment. One of them was to contact Johnny Eacret at the PX Ranch, a cow-calf operation north of town. Hearing that the ranch owner was Bing Crosby didn't bother him a bit. "Hells fire," he

Bing decides to hit the hay.

Above: Uncle Bing always got plenty of mail, even at the ranch. Below: Mail call.

said to himself, "a job's a job." Finding a place to eat and spend the night was easy, but finding the ranch was going to be another matter. "What the hell; sometimes ya just gotta let the guts go with the feathers," he mumbled, as he fired up the Chevy and headed north to the PX. He almost missed the turnoff to the ranch, because his thoughts were drifting away from Idaho and into Nevada.

The main road led TJ to the heart of the action and the sign that read "PX Ranch." A teenage boy was walking toward him from the barn and TJ asked him where he could find the ranch foreman. "Johnny's in the house with my dad," said the boy, pointing to the bungalow with a white fence. Just about the time TJ parked his truck, he saw a cowboy in a clean shirt and Levi's standing on the front porch; he figured this must be the ranch boss.

It didn't take long for Johnny to hire TJ after he heard the man's war stories and sensed his eagerness to work on a cattle ranch again. The newly-employed cowboy found his way to the bunkhouse, brought in his bed roll, rifle, and saddle. He felt right at home.

It would be several months later, during my summer vacation, that Mother and I went to visit Uncle Bing at his PX Ranch and I met TJ.

After we had settled in, I went about exploring the place. Much as I had expected, there was a main house, barn, cook house, horse corrals, and sleeping quarters for the wranglers. I was anxious to check out the horses and see if I would be allowed to ride one. Although my uncle had said we could make ourselves at home there, I wasn't sure if that included riding lessons for me. When I spoke to my mother about it the next morning, she suggested that I wait until supper time when the ranch manager would be sitting at our table. Johnny Eacret had the last word on things there at the PX, except for Uncle Bing, of course; he made all the major decisions.

I waited until I thought the time was right, just before the apple pie and coffee refills came around, to approach Johnny. I asked him if I had his permission to ride one of the horses, and if so, which one would be best for me. He responded by asking me the dreaded question in return: "Did you ever ride a horse before, Carolyn"? When I said, "Just a couple of times. I know I'm supposed to get up on the left side of the horse." The man had every right to laugh at me but didn't; instead, he just smiled a nodded his head as if to say "I understand."

"Tell you what," Johnny began, "why don't you go and look up TJ tomorrow morning out at the stables; I'll tell him to set you up." He took a sip of his coffee and then started in on the pie.

I was up and out like a shot the next morning, grabbed some toast and an apple from the kitchen, then headed for the stables. A man came out of one of the stalls leading a gray and white mare. When he saw me he stopped, took off his sweat-stained cowboy hat and shielded his eyes from the early morning sun. "You must be Mr. Bing's niece," he said. "And you must be TJ," I replied. Not a very auspicious beginning for pupil and riding instructor, but there it was. Besides, as I was to learn later on, TJ was not a man of fancy words. He stood a fair amount taller than I, yet not a big man, except for what he referred to as his "beer belly." As most cowboys do, TJ wore a wide leather belt that had molded to the shape of his body and was fastened with a dingy silver buckle, a token of some rodeo event of days gone by.

He reached in his pocket and produced one of those red bandana handkerchiefs, which had definitely seen better days. Even though it was faded and some loose threads were in evidence, it did the job as he swiped it across his forehead. He replaced his hat and I had the feeling he was taking his time to size me up.

"You done any ridin' before, little lady?" he asked.

"Just a few times," I replied.

"Well, let's see what ya got," he said. TJ bent over slightly, and using his hands, he interlaced his fingers to form a human stirrup for me. Putting my left foot into his cupped hands and reaching for the saddle horn, I made a short jump, just as TJ pushed up on my other foot. Between that and my own momentum, I almost flew over the top of the horse, but I grabbed the trusty saddle horn and landed where I was supposed to be. John Wayne makes it look so easy.

The gray and white mare that had been standing by patiently was chosen to be my faithful steed that day. TJ held the reins and led the horse out into the corral while I hung on for dear life. We paraded around like that for a while until TJ felt I was comfortable astride the dappled mare,

Rosie. For the next couple of days, I only went riding under the vigilant eye of my trainer and stayed within earshot. It was as if he were teaching me to drive a car, rather than how to ride a horse, the way TJ made every move seem important. Instead of "put on the brake," he would say "pull back on the reins." "Dig in your heels," meant "step on the gas." Luckily, Rosie and I passed inspection by the third day. After that, TJ and I would go riding almost every morning. That way he could check on the feed and water troughs at the ranch, I could become a better rider, and not be by myself. Once the ride was over and we were back at the barn, TJ would take out his Buck knife and cut my ever-present apple in half for Rosie and me.

Uncle Bing arrived at the PX about two weeks after Mother and I did. He drove his light green Cadillac with white sidewall tires into the yard and in front of the main house. Johnny helped him unload his things from the car, and then we all sat in the front room while Johnny gave his boss a report on the ranch. I was itching to show off my new found horsemanship to my uncle, but knew I had to wait for the adults to complete their conversation. Bing gave Mother his news from home, saying that Dixie was re-doing the living room and had hired an interior decorator. "The guy was driving me nuts," Bing said. "I couldn't wait to get up here." At last it was my turn to strut my stuff. Uncle Bing stood on the porch with Mother as I took Rosie for a spin. They both applauded my performance, and then Bing called out to me, "you should try to be a barrel racer at the Silver State Stampede next year, Carolyn." I couldn't tell if that was an invitation or just a compliment, but it was sure nice to hear.

That summer was another memorable one, thanks to Uncle Bing and a likeable old cowboy they called TJ.

49

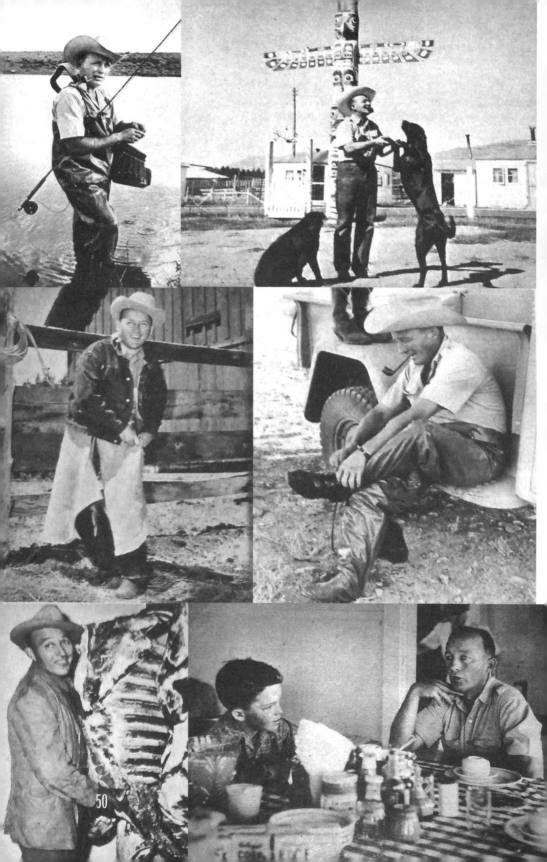

ELKO

Bing and the boys: Gary, now 20, Philip and Dennis, 19, and Lindsay, 15.

51

Welcome
to
His Honor

Bing Crosby

•

The Whole Durn City

Chapter Three:
I'm An Old Cowhand

THE IDEA OF A MULTIMEDIA STAR THE CALIBER OF BING CROSBY adopting a small town in northern Nevada sounds much like a fairy tale. Yet this was far from being a case of the handsome prince and the lowly maiden, but rather, it is the story of a man being true to himself. As a result, the town adopted him.

From the time he bought his first ranch near Elko in 1943 until five years later when he was made honorary mayor, Uncle Bing spent his leisure time in the area hunting and fishing. Bing's career was going full tilt during that period, including being named the top moneymaking star for the fourth straight year, which meant that vacation time away from filming, recording, and radio shows was limited. He was able to arrange his own schedule, however, in order to be with his four sons during the summer months at one of his ranches. As his visits became more frequent, the townspeople grew to know him as a local rancher rather than some kind of superstar. His demeanor was casual and friendly, not uppity and demanding. He became a familiar face around the town, especially at places like the DuPont Pharmacy, which not only carried the usual drugstore items, but also had a lunch counter that served fountain specialties. Located at Fourth and Idaho Streets, DuPont's was a popular locals place. It had twenty stools for seating at the counter and you would find them filled almost any day of the week from eleven in the morning until one-thirty, when the lunch crowd would leave.

Bing was a regular customer, not on a daily basis, but whenever he was in town, DuPont's was one of his favorite stopping places. He would climb onto a stool, rest his elbows on the counter and reach for a menu. The customary patrons knew the food selections by heart, but there was always a chance something new had been added, so it was wise to always check the menu, just in case. One particular day was a hot one, and Bing stopped in for a cold drink and sat on one of the empty stools. When the waitress came by, Uncle Bing ordered a vanilla milkshake. "I'm busy with another order right now," the waitress said, "I'll fix it for you in a minute." He said that would be OK. To help pass the time, Bing left his place at the counter and walked over to the public scale which was standing in the corner. He put in a penny and waited to see the numbers, telling him how much he weighed. Satisfied with the results, he started to whistle as he returned to his stool at the counter. When she heard that familiar sound, the waitress realized who it was and could have died of embarrassment; she had told Bing Crosby to "wait a minute." That scene was typical of how Uncle Bing was regarded in Elko, and it's just the way he wanted it to be. No fuss, no special treatment, just one of the guys.

Being well-known and well-liked also had other advantages. One day Bing came into DuPont's for a snack before heading back to his ranch in Tuscarora. He finished eating, paid the bill, and went out the door. A few minutes after he left, the waitress found his pipe still sitting on the counter. She knew it was too late to try and catch him, so she just set it up on top of the cash register, knowing that he would remember where he left it. Sure enough, about an hour later Bing returned to retrieve his beloved pipe, even though he was halfway back to the ranch when he discovered it missing.

By all accounts, my uncle fit in with the people of Elko County so well that after knowing him and working with him for four years, he was asked to become honorary mayor of the town. Newt Crumley was the most well-known man in Elko, but Bing Crosby was the most well-known man in the world. He was notified by telegram that the city supervisors had officially voted to give him that honor. He never ran for political office and my guess is, the word "honorary" peaked his interest enough to consider the offer. As soon as he accepted, the local residents, ranchers, and businessmen began forming committees to handle the celebration.

Chapter Three: *I'm An Old Cowhand*

For Uncle Bing, it was another accolade in his already fabulous career. The 1940s belonged to him; he had won the coveted Oscar for his acting talent, had several No. 1 selling records, was the top box office draw in films, and was setting a new standard for radio performances. But this was different; being asked to become Elko's honorary mayor was the "city family" reaching out to him. These were folks that he bought supplies from at the hay and feed store. There was Mary who made him a milkshake at DuPont's, and John who went hunting with him. People who liked him, accepted him as a fellow rancher and concerned citizen, and wanted him to be involved in their community. This honor was very special, and it was an appointment to serve ad infinitum.

When the news became known to the public regarding Bing's honorary mayor ceremony, many people sent congratulatory telegrams, including Nevada state officials, such as Senator George Malone: "Convey my congratulations to Bing Crosby for the high spirit of cooperation and friendliness he has expressed since his first arrival in Elko county, a world-renowned figure who has retained a sincere feeling of neighborliness for his fellow man." Governor Vail Pittman: "You have measured up to those fine attributes which characterize a true Nevadan and I know that your neighbors and friends in Elko wish to show you this recognition as a testimonial of their friendship and appreciation."

This was high praise indeed.

Faster than you could snap your fingers, committees met to pool their ideas for a real bang-up tribute to their man of the hour. A couple of ideas were shot down before the meetings were over, but finally it was agreed that Newt Crumley and Al Manhan should "tackle this job by the horns and wrestle it to the ground." This was language that everyone could understand and both men gladly accepted their assignment.

At the next meeting, all of the volunteers voted on the proposed plans and submitted them to Dave Dotta, the Mayor. There would be speeches, of course, and Dotta would present Bing with a key to the city. Saturday, February 7th was to be designated "Bing Crosby Day" in Elko. The festivities would be held in two parts: an afternoon presentation, followed by a banquet in the evening which would be paid for by ticket sales.

The question of what locale could accommodate the crowds was easily answered.

Elko resident Newt Crumley, who practically owned the town, became a great friend to Uncle Bing. Not only did he sell some of his own ranch property to his friend, but he was also instrumental later on in obtaining the famous denim tuxedos, organizing events that included Uncle Bing, and donated his time and money to local causes. Newt was very civic-minded and well-liked by both the townspeople and ranchers. Besides, he owned two hotels. Problem solved. His Ranchinn would be the scene of the mayoral ceremony, and the Commercial Hotel the banquet site.

In the days leading up to the big shebang, the newspaper was full of doom and gloom, talking about a possible storm front coming in, bringing rain and maybe even some snow. By Tuesday, four days prior to the ceremonies, the sky looked threatening and there was some concern in town about the weather. But Elko was in a festive mood and people were determined that nothing was going to put a damper on Der Bingle's red-letter day.

For once, the weatherman was right; the storm that had been predicted and it was on its way. The rain was a mixed blessing, but in any case, the city families were prepared. The published report was good news for Reno, as that area was facing the worst water shortage in forty years. While rain and snow flurries slowly moved eastward, it was a lead pipe cinch that it would hit Elko later in the day.

Uncle Bing and his wife, my aunt Dixie, arrived from Los Angeles during a brief snowfall on Tuesday, and Bing was quoted as saying that although he couldn't take credit for bringing the storm with him from California, he was grateful for the moisture, because it was badly needed. Every rancher in the county knew the value of a decent rain.

The Crosbys stayed in town for awhile and met with some of the committee members to go over the plans for the big event on Saturday. Bing had received numerous awards and honors during the years of his career, but never one like this. It would be the first time he would become an honorary mayor, and as such, the first man in Nevada history to be so appointed.

Chapter Three: *I'm An Old Cowhand*

After conferring with Newt Crumley and Al Manhan, plus several other committee people, Bing and Dixie drove up to their North Fork Ranch.

Wednesday in Elko was spent making preparations behind the scenes. Ranchinn had a full house and an ace in the hole; not only was every hotel room booked, but also the official ceremony for Bing was scheduled to take place there. Microphones were being put in place, and the courtyard in front of the hotel was swept about every hour in anticipation of a big crowd. The only thing missing was a red carpet.

On Thursday, as if to ward off the clouds and the cold, a bunch of fellows from the Jaycees built a bonfire in front of Manhan's store in the middle of the street and brewed coffee. It was barely sunup when folks started gathering around the fire to discuss the plans for the day. One of the young men in a cowboy hat said, "maybe Hollywood would send up some cameramen, and we might be in the Movietone newsreels." "Aw don't be a sap," said his friend Wesley; "those people don't care about Elko."

They finished their coffee in silence, but it was obvious that the prospect of the town gaining national notoriety only added to the excitement in those early hours.

The first tickets to the banquet were going to be limited to members of the various Elko civic clubs and their guests, one each. This included: the Exchange, Rotary, Lions, Chamber of Commerce and the Junior Chamber. After that, ticket sales would be open to the general public.

Reporters at the local newspaper were fond of calling him "Der Bingle." Of course, everyone knew who they meant, and he liked it; it was a term of affection. The paper ran the story about the banquet plans; "three bucks a plate" it read. But there was a surprise announcement; when Bing heard about it, "this party is on me," he said. The committee told him that they were planning to sell 360 tickets to the dinner. Bing said that was okay, and that he still was going to pick up the check.

Manhan's clothing store was to be the site of ticket sales, and about a hundred people were waiting in line even before the 10 a.m. opening of the store. When Al Manhan made the announcement of Bing's generos-

Bing goes shopping at the Mercantile in Elko.

ity, the response from the crowd was such a loud cheer that they didn't even hear the whistle of the train going by on its way to Reno.

Bing drove into town again on Thursday to pick up some supplies that were needed at the ranch and then he stopped in at the Mercantile to buy a hat. This was another place that he frequented; he liked it because it carried just about everything, especially Red Wing Shoes and Wolverine boots. It was turning colder now and the locals were keeping a sharp eye on the temperature as well as road conditions. After making a few stops to buy the things on his shopping list, Uncle Bing headed for the Commercial Hotel. He pulled into a parking spot on the street and went through the front entrance.

The Commercial Hotel was a popular watering hole and gathering place; today, however, it was busier than usual. Bing was looking for a couple of committee members to ask them about the seating arrangements for the banquet. He figured his best chance of running them down would be at the bar.

Chapter Three: *I'm An Old Cowhand*

Walking through the casino section of the hotel, Bing noticed that there was no shortage of gambling patrons; a couple of them looked up as he passed by and said, "Hi, Bing." He gave them the "hi" sign in return as he looked down the rows of slot machines, but didn't see hide nor hair of the men he was looking for.

It seemed as though everyone in the place was smoking, mostly cigarettes, some of them the roll-your-own-kind, too. Even the fellows over at the pool tables had cigarettes lit and would puff on them in between shots. When it was time for a player to chalk his pool cue, he would just let the cigarette dangle from his mouth. There is very little protocol when playing pool or billiards, and having a smoke and a beer is all part of playing the game. Uncle Bing liked the atmosphere there, being with other men and blending in to their world. He was tempted to stay and shoot a little eight-ball, but after checking the time on his favorite Bulova, thought better of it and moved on to continue his search.

A couple of cowboys were sitting at the bar having a beer and playing liar's dice. The country-western music was going full blast, so Bing had to wait until the bartender came within earshot to ask about the men in question. He was hoping not to be recognized, because he didn't like the looks of the guy sitting alone down at the end of the bar on the last stool. The man looked out of place there. Wearing a pork-pie hat, sport coat and slacks, he was definitely over dressed for the Commercial. Bing had him pegged as a news reporter from one of the bigger cities, maybe Reno or Salt Lake City. In any case, this was no place for an interview or photo shoot with Bing in a bar, and a casino in the background. He checked around the rest of the area, including the coffee shop, but there was no sign of any committee members.

As he started to leave, Uncle Bing ran into his friend Newt Crumley and they chewed the fat for awhile about the upcoming Bing Crosby Day and the probability of bad weather. Newt told Bing that Jack and John Hunter, owners of the Hunter theatre, had contacted the committee and offered the use of their theatre (free of charge) in case Bing's event could not be held outdoors at Ranchinn. The Hunters also arranged to show the regular Saturday afternoon movie matinee at ten in the morning in order to clear the way for Der Bingle. It seemed as though the entire town was pitching in to show Uncle Bing how pleased they were to have him as their honorary mayor. They wanted the event to be nearly perfect; it was a real love affair. The upcoming ceremony and festivities dominated the local paper all week and the newspaper did a land-office business. The occasion was so rare and so popular that it caused quite a number of stores and shops in town to take out paid advertising in the special section of the paper, or to send a message of congratulations. Apparently the local government even got in on the act. On page three of the February 7th edition was a full page tribute to the prospective mayor, complete with photo that stated: "Welcome to His Honor Bing Crosby (from) The Whole Durn City." Referred to as the "singing star of stage and screen," Bing was always front page news.

"Today is Bing Crosby Day in Elko," read the banner across the top of the front page of the *Elko Daily Free Press* on February 7, 1948. Then: "Crosby is Honorary Mayor" (in a one-inch size headline). Uncle Bing must have felt very lucky on that day. It was like hitting a hole-in-one at Pebble Beach.

Al Manhan was chairman of "Bing Crosby Day" and at two o'clock that Saturday he presented District Attorney A. L. Puccinelli, who was master of ceremonies. Next came Newt Crumley who presented Bing to Mayor Dotta by saying: "He is a world figure; his presence is sought all over the world. He's a wonderful fellow and we are very fortunate to have him confer this honor on us today."

Several hundred people were on hand in the courtyard of the Ranchinn that afternoon to welcome Uncle Bing as honorary mayor of Elko. The actual mayor, Dave Dotta, conducted the ceremony as the crowd smiled in approval. Dotta's remarks, while conferring the honorary position, included phrases such as: "outstanding contributions to American citizenship" (perhaps referring to Bing's fundraising for the war effort). He was also complimented on his sportsmanship, parenthood, clean living, and success in the field of entertainment. "We are grateful," the mayor continued, "for your contributions to the city and county of Elko." Everyone applauded in agreement.

It was obvious that the residents of this small town held Uncle Bing in high regard. When he introduced his wife, Dixie, to the audience, they gave her the same warm reception that had been given to him. This was a very generous gesture on their part, because the townspeople knew that Aunt Dixie seldom came to Elko; she didn't like it much. As the ceremony continued, some of the local dignitaries and businessmen chimed in with Mayor Dotta's remarks, saying what a fine fellow Bing was and how proud they were to have him associated with their fair city. One of the men commented on the fact that Frank Sinatra had become honorary mayor of Palm Springs. Bing scoffed at the idea and remarked that Sinatra was no cowboy and probably had not even put cuffs on his Levi jeans. This line got quite a laugh.

After he had accepted the scroll of office and thanked everyone, Bing said he learned that the city was trying to build a new swimming pool to replace the old one. Right then and there he announced his donation of $5,000 to get the project going.

Before the close of the affair, Mayor Dotta presented Bing with the key to the city. The message on the oversized key read: "Bing Crosby, Honorary Mayor, Elko, Nevada. The Town is yours." The mayor also let Bing know that this new position would also include a certain amount of work by saying, "you'll have little time left for your comparatively unimportant job of making motion pictures."

Following congratulations all around, the crowd dispersed to await the banquet at seven o'clock held at the Commercial Hotel in both the Lounge and the Brand Room.

The banquet that evening was a monumental occasion by Elko standards. Uncle Bing looked very official in his dark suit and somber expression while holding the large cardboard key to the city. I'm not sure if he was disappointed over the fact that the key wasn't genuine, or because he forgot to wear a hat over his bald head. Aunt Dixie, on the other hand, looked the part of a celebrity's wife in her fox fur jacket.

The party lasted for several hours and Bing sang a couple of songs. Near the end of the evening, Uncle Bing made the rounds in the Lounge and the Brand Room, shaking hands and thanking people for his newly-elected post.

Soon after being granted this special honor, there came another one for Bing. His latest picture with Bob Hope, *Road to Rio,* be-

As wife Dixie Lee looks on, Bing accepts the key to the city.

came the top box office film for 1948. His mother, my grandma, said she was proud of his achievement, even though he didn't play the part of a priest this time.

When the weekend celebration was over, the Crosbys headed back to southern California and warmer weather.

Bing and Dixie returned to Elko at the end of June to attend the rodeo, the Silver State Stampede.

Take Me Back to My Boots and Saddle

Beginning in the 1930s when his career really took over most of his life, Uncle Bing still made sure he had some leisure time. His hectic schedule of recording, filming, and regular radio broadcasts were enough to keep three men busy, yet my uncle could somehow squeeze in time for at least nine holes of golf, a baseball game, or a trip to Elko. Then, when duty called, in the form of a parade and rodeo in that Nevada town, the honorary mayor was quick to respond.

Chapter Three: *I'm An Old Cowhand*

The Silver State Stampede rodeo was a big event for the people of Elko County. Over the years it had become a stop-and-start affair, but as of 1948, it had not taken place in thirteen years. There had been a few ideas tossed around on how to restore the rodeo, but they never really got off the ground until Uncle Bing came along. Now that they had an honorary mayor who was an international celebrity, and a rancher to boot, it must have been just the ticket the rodeo committee was looking for. There's nothing like having a famous singing cowboy to kick-start your Stampede. Maybe thirteen was a lucky number after all. The long absence of this cowboy competition made it an anniversary the whole town was waiting for.

Bing had been crowned "his honor" only a few months before when he received word in Los Angeles that his presence was requested; the people of Elko wanted him to be part of their Stampede event. Once he said he would clear his calendar and dust off his boots, they knew he would be there. Luckily he was between pictures, having completed *The Emperor Waltz* and preparing to film *A Connecticut Yankee in King Arthur's Court*. Apparently recordings could wait a while.

The grand opening of the Stampede was scheduled for Friday, June 25, 1948. It had been an interesting year so far; the livestock market was steady, Tom Dewey was governor of Pennsylvania and fighter Joe Lewis lost his heavyweight title to Jersey Joe Walcott. And now with the rodeo starting up again, this was even more front page news.

To begin the festivities on that special day was a parade starting at 12:30, led by Bing and Newt Crumley. Photos of the occasion show Uncle Bing riding a horse and sporting his finest western wear, including chaps. There was no shortage of parade entries, and competition was fierce in the various categories to be judged; each one wanted to take home a prize. Mostly involving horses and equipment, it was the best parade in years, everyone said. The stores on Idaho Street put red, white, and blue bunting out in front, just like the Fourth of July. It was one of those "red letter" days again and Uncle Bing was front and center. It was such a huge event, in fact, that the *Elko Daily Free Press* had a section of their paper printed in green ink — Green Streak Souvenir Edition — it said. "Bing Crosby to Open Silver State Stampede" was the headline at

Crosby Is

"Der Bingle" Welcomed By City Family at Afternoon Ceremonies

...'s heart today as he was
...held at Ranchinn.
...ent.

Elko took Bin...
made "Honorary N...
Hundreds of peop...

The honor was co...
Crosby by Mayor...
when he said, "We...
this honor upon...
cause of your out...
butions to Amer...
sportsmanship, c...
living and the f...
ment.

"We are grat...
tributions to t...
of Elko.

"Because o...
take great ple...
upon you the...
Mayor of th...

Bing acce...
words, "T...
I appreciate...
remarks...
wish I d...

Bing...
accomp...
mer D...

"I k...
count...
pledg...
where...

If...
Bing introduced his wife, who
acccompanied him to Elko, the for-
said mer Dixie L...

"I know that the people of Elko...
try county mean what they say. I...
"I pledge my support to help you...
whenever I can."

It was at this point that Bing...
Knoll he understood the city was
trying trying to build a swimming pool.
"I used the one you have and
know you need a new one," he
said. "I'd like to drop $5,000 in
the kitty for your new one."

Then he added, "that's one five
Uncle Sam will not get."

As Allen Carter had made reference to the honorary mayor of
Palm Springs, Crosby made the
observation: "I figured those
dudes would pick a dud.
And with disdain, "Some cowboy."

The man who was described by
Newton Crumley as the best liked man in the world today thanked the people who had attended
the ceremony officially and great
person which gathered for the occasion.

His closing remarks were,
"Well, there's lots of work to be
done and its getting cold. In
case the mayor wants to go on a
vacation all he'll need to do is
to call on me and I'll be glad to
take over."

Today Is Bing Crosby's Day In

Elko Daily Free Press

Largest Circulation of any Newspaper Published in Eastern Nevada— Published Every Afternoon Except Sunday

SIXTY SIXTH YEAR   No. 31   ELKO, ELKO COUNTY, NEVADA   SATURDAY, FEBRUARY 7, 1948

Crosby Is Honorary Ma...

"Der Bingle" Welcomed By City Family at Afternoon Ceremonies

Elko took Bing Crosby to its heart today as he was
made "Honorary Mayor" at a ceremony held at Ranchinn.
Hundreds of people were present to witness the event.

The honor was conferred upon
Crosby by Mayor David Dotta
when he said, "We are conferring
this honor upon you today because of your outstanding contributions to American citizenship,
sportsmanship, parenthood, clean
living and the field of entertainment.

"We are grateful for your contributions to the city and county
of Elko.

"Because of these things, I
take great pleasure in conferring
upon you the title of 'Honorary
Mayor of the City of Elko.'"

Bing accepted the honor with the
words, "Thank you for this scroll,
I appreciate the sincerity of the
remarks made here today. I only
wish I deserved this honor."

Crosby's, then presented Bing
to Mayor David Dotta after which
the official confirmation was
made.

"He is a world figure," said
Crumley to the listening crowd.
"His presence is sought all over
the world. We are happy he likes
us and we know that we like
him. He is a wonderful fellow and
we are very fortunate to have
him confer this honor on us today."

When Mayor Dotta handed the
scroll to Bing he said, "You'll
have little time left for your comparatively unimportant job of
making motion pictures."

CONGRATULATIONS all ar-
ound followed and the crowd dispersed. Bing took time out this
afternoon to visit a number of
Elko residents in their places of
business becoming personally
acquainted with them.

A program of fun was being
prepared for the evening's celebration in the Lounge and Brand
Room of the Commercial hotel,
with the banquet set to start at
7 o'clock.

Gate Bridge Claims 90th Jump Victim

SAN FRANCISCO, Feb. 7—(UP)
—Famed Golden Gate Bridge
claimed its 90th victim today, but
for the first time the victim had
wanted to live.

Alfred (Dusty) Rhodes, 38, Hollywood stunt man and movie double, tore away from two wh...
workers yesterday and leaped 265
feet to his death in the bay be...
A coast guard boat fished his
body from the water 20 minutes
later.

Rhodes made his leap for the
sake of publicity. He had planned
it for five months.

The fall did not cause his death,
even though it is equal to drop-
ping off a 25 story building. An
autopsy showed that Rhodes
drowned. He suffered only mi-
nor internal injuries from hitting...

Cold Wave Is Sweeping Down From Northwest

By United Press

Two separate cold waves were
sweeping into the country early
today; one west of the Rocky
Mountains along the Pacific coast
and the other to the east of the
mountains in the north central
states.

The cold air mass moving along
the west coast came out of Alas-
ka, carrying with it a heavy
snow and rain storm. Forecast-
ers said it threatened to engulf
the citrus groves of southern California.

The other cold wave came down
from the Yukon creeping into the
weather...
it for ...
The fall did ...
even though it is equal to drop-
ping off a 25 story building.
autopsy showed that Rhodes
drowned. He suffered only mi-
nor internal injuries from hitting...

Prices Drop... ...es Of Nation...

IS DEFEAT 57 TO 22; ...E TONIGHT

...invading basketball team
...a score of 57 to 22. A sec-
...tonight by the Elko and...

Humboldt County Reconsidering ...as Tax

WINNEMUCCA, Nev. Feb. 7—
(UP)—Humboldt county has join-
...the list of Nevada counties
which the re-considering the additional one and one-half cent gaso-
line tax to bolster road revenue...
...was disclosed today.

The 1947 legislature enacted the
...w, providing that counties could
...dd one and one-half cents a gal-
...n tax on existing state levies
...n a voluntary basis. Revenue
...rom the added levy are to be
...ed only for highway construc-
...on and maintenance and was to
...divided between cities and
...county on the basis of the respec-
...ve assessed valuation.

Clark county is now reconsider-
...ing the added levy. Both Hum-
...boldt and Clark county turned
...the tax down after the legislature
adjourned. The Clark county
...grand jury recommended adop-
...tion of the levy to provide funds
...for street improvement.

Omar Bradley Is New Chief Of Staff Today

WASHINGTON, Feb. 7 (UP)—
Gen. Dwight D. Eisenhower, who
steps down today as army chief
of staff, disclosed that he will
forego a fishing vacation to begin work immediately on his
memoirs.

Eisenhower told a farewell
news-conference at the Pentagon
that he wanted to "provide some...

"Its T... Me" Sa... On Mar...

Commu...
Trend M...
Or Crash...

CHICAGO, F...
tail prices on fo...
in scattered spot...
try but experts...
early to tell whe...
...s resulted from...
plunges on the...
...commodity, live...
...ties markets.
Corn, wheat, o...
...hogs skidded do...
...yesterday on the b...

WASHINGTON,
A month ago tod...
...of agriculture Cli...
...derson received a...
Frank Anderson,...
...the Anderson Labo...
Brooklyn, Mass...
The agriculture...
...road is chuckled, a...
...able to bring it ba...
...on Feb. 6. He repo...
...his desk again yes...
...informed him that...
...laboratories was...
...month ago.
"Commodity prices...
...upon a prolonged de...
...ginning on or abou...
1948."

...the Chicago grain e...
...oats failed to drop the...
...permissible during...
...trading...

SECRETARY of agric...
Clinton P. Anderson sai...
...market break... "it's too fas...

"I don't think a soul...
...it stands it," he added.
On Capitol Hill, chairman...
...ford E. Hope, R., Kans., of...
House Agriculture comm...
...said he'd be "surprised if th...
...ket doesn't bounce back."
Economist Roger W. Bab...

Der Bingle Takes the Check for 360 Banquet Guests Saturday

Crosbys Arrive In Elko Prior To Ceremonies

Crooner Will Have to Work For Mayoralty

"The party's all right, but it's got to be on me," said Bing Crosby, who'll soon be the honorary mayor of Elko.

He arrived in Elko this morning with his wife, the former Dixie Lee, and stopped here a short time before going to his ranch, on the North Fork.

Committee members told Bing that 360 persons would be able to attend the banquet in his honor at The Lounge and Brand Room of the Commercial hotel Saturday night. "That's okay," said Bing, "but I want them all there as my guests."

* * *

ABOUT THAT time, 100 or more persons were milling about in front of Manhan's waiting for the tickets to go on sale at three bucks a plate. It was almost 10 o'clock, deadline for the sale to commence. The news of Bing's decision and generous offer rushed to ticket announcement. onse was so ting its way to

WHO WAS th body'll know, re present, 20 small hours uld have been t to Elko. The ked up the de ting last nigh fire in the t et, brewed so d to keep war cury was not se of the storm he Daily Free er was on han on and snapped release.

dications cont Bing's going the hard way. a was in Salt L still insisting th oing to have c directin' p a street or tw (Continued on

Nevada Officials Wire Crosby Congratulations On Honor Of Being Made Honorary Mayor

Nevada's officials were among the many who wired Bing Crosby congratulations when his appointment as honorary mayor of Elko became generally known. Some of the samples of wires received, copies of which were forwarded to the local committee, follow:

Sen. George W. Malone— "Regret I will not be able to be in Elko Saturday for official appointment of Bing Crosby as honorary mayor since I am to be guest speaker at the annual Sowbelly dinner of the Colorado Mining Association in Denver on that night.

"Please express my appreciation to the city and congratulations to the residents at your ceremonies upon their timely recognition of a man who has shown himself to be exemplary of the American way of life. Convey my congratulations to Bing Crosby for the high spirit of cooperation and friendliness he has expressed since his first arrival in Elko county, a world renowned figure who has retained a sin-

McCarran, wired regrets for him, as senator now en route Denver.

* * *

Gov. Vail Pittman— "My hearty congratulations to you upon being appointed honorary mayor of Elko. I am pleased that you have accepted this unique appointment. You have measured up to those fine attributes which characterize a true Nevadan and I know that your neighbors and friends in Elko wish to show you this recognition as a testimonial of their friendship and affection. Sorry indeed that I will be unable to be in Elko for ceremony on Saturday. I have made definite arrangements to be in Denver at that time to attend mining conference."

* * *

Others wiring regrets being unable to attend included:

Francis R. (Tank) Smith, Mayor of Reno—"Bing is a wonderful guy."

Charles H. Russell, Representative in Congress— "Regards to all present who gather er to honor one of Elko Coun

Much-Needed Moisture Brou State By Storm

Snow Falls Fa Furiously Her For Short Time

The storm which swept i the west today blanketed t tion with a light fall of Snow fell furiously here short time this morning an cations were that it was up at higher levels. The late was welcomed here, but th dampening factor was th mediate prospects for muc snow looked dim.

RENO, Feb. 5 (UP)— threat of the worst water age in 40 years was all partially today by a mod heavy storm which left fr inches to four feet of sr the Sierra Nevadas and t Rose-Lake Tahoe areas.

Only one inch of snow Reno during the night w flurries and st for today a was still fall tions in the vith two feet ted in the and from th he summit. T ay was clos irass Lake o

RM was ard and Nort f new snow. 'innemucca rig at 10 A. pected to hi in the day.

ghway depa ches of new er Summit d on highw lake to Gold lains from t e. The depa hes of sno nopah and ar Creek hi

RE requir om Bridgs steady sr at area. required highway

Bing Crosby To Be Named Honorary Mayor of Elko Saturday Afternoon

Bing Crosby, singing star of the stage and screen, will be officially named "honorary mayor of Elko," Saturday afternoon at 2 o'clock, at a public ceremony, which will be held in the courtyard of Ranchinn.

Bing accepted the honor Sunday and since then has informed local committees that he will be here for the ceremony Saturday.

A banquet will be held in his honor at the Commercial hotel, Saturday night at 7 o'clock. Members of the committee regret the fact that the banquet cannot be opened to the public generally and have, of necessity, limited the occasion to members of the various Elko civic clubs and their guests. Each member of the Exchange, Rotary, Lions, Elko chamber of commerce and Elko junior chamber of commerce will be limited to one guest each.

Tickets for the banquet will go on sale at Manhan's Thursday morning at 10 o'clock. Banquet tickets will be $3 each. A rapid sale is being anticipated.

There will be 210 banquet tickets available for The Lounge, with 100 available for Brand Room. Ceremonies conducted in The Lounge will be heard in the Brand Room and Crosby will make a personal appearance in the Brand Room, following The Lounge ceremony.

Tickets will be held on a first come, first serve basis." Those getting the first tickets will be admitted to The Lounge, while the additional 100

tickets will be for the Brand Room.

The singing star accepted the mayorship Sunday after being advised by telegram that the city supervisors had officially voted him that honor.

Crosby, owner of extensive ranch property in Elko county and who has made numerous friends upon his visitors to Elko, will be officially appointed by Mayor David Dotta of Elko at the public ceremony scheduled for Saturday afternoon.

Mayor Dotta officially proclaimed Saturday, Feb. 7, as "Bing Crosby Day in Elko."

Crosby is the first man ever to hold appointment as honorary mayor of Elko, and as far as is known, is the first honorary mayor appointed by any Nevada municipality. Governor Vail Pittman, Mayor Smith of Reno, and Mayor Craigan of Las Vegas have been invited to be present.

Mayor Dotta's telegram to Crosby advising him of his appointment said, "In humble recognition of your outstanding contribution to a high standard of American citizenship, sportsmanship, clean living, parenthood, et al, and finally, your substantial additions to community life in the city and county of Elko, I am privileged and proud to herewith appoint you, by official proclamation, honorary mayor of the city of Elko, Nevada, to serve ad infinitum. We are grateful that you have seen fit to accept this honor."

Bing Crosby To Open Silver State Stam[pede]

World's Finest [Ri]ders To Be [Fe]atured In Rodeo

★ ★ ★   Green Streak Souvenir Edition —   ★ ★ ★

Elko Daily Free Press

Largest Circulation of any Newspaper Published in Eastern Nevada—Published Every Afternoon Except Sunday

SIXTY-NINTH YEAR   No. 147   ELKO, ELKO COUNTY, NEVADA, Wednesday, June 23, 1948   FIRST SE[CTION]

Stop Governor Dewey Drive

Rain Causes Louis-Walcott Heavyweight Title Fight to Be Postponed

NEW YORK, June 23 (?)—
Because of rain, the 25th Club has today postponed the Joe Louis-Jersey Joe Walcott heavyweight title fight at Yankee Stadium until tomorrow night. It had been scheduled for tonight.

If additional postponements are necessary Friday night and Saturday night are available at the Stadium.

To keep the spectators entertained, and the show moving along at a swift pace, special performers from Sorenson's show will be on hand to do their stuff.

(Continued on Page 8)

...[column text]...

NONORARY MAYOR OF ELKO WILL OPEN STAMPEDE FRIDAY JUNE 25th

66

"Let 'er Buck", Says Bing as First Rodeo in 13 Years Opens

More Than 3,000 On Hand to See Tish-Roarin' Show Today, Sunday Winds Up Stampede

"Let 'er buck!"

With these words Bing Crosby, honorary mayor of Elko, rang up the curtain on the opening day of the Silver State Stampede at the fairgrounds yesterday at 1 o'clock.

Some 3,300 people, including many from out of town, were on hand to witness the first rodeo held here in 13 years. It was a show they will not soon forget. Under the direction of J. C. Martin, famed rodeo producer, a galaxy of contesting and featured performers put on a show which was characterized by roarin' action, fast riding. The spectacular feature performance gave plenty of thrills and not a dull moment in the two and a half hour program.

* * *

FOLLOWING the brilliant entry of cowboys and cowgirls, in which 100 horses paraded in close-leader form about the arena, Newton Crumley, of the Commercial hotel, introduced distinguished guests from parts of the state, Utah, and who graced the opening ceremonies with their presence.

To be remembered most, the proceedings will depend, of course, on individual taste. Certainly the main part of the program was the demonstrations of riding techniques displayed by nationally famous cowboys. The "money" part of the hanging from bareback riding, through calf riding, steer wrestling, to tough Brahma bulls, professional contestants really had the stands on edge, a full feet in their demonstrations of the art of rodeo.

Visitor to Elko Passes Away at General Hospital

Mrs. Emma Thatcher Jeppesen, mother of Mrs. William Thorpe, died this morning at the Elko general hospital after an illness of two weeks. She had been visiting in Elko the past three

Laszlo Varga Murder Trial Opens Monday Morning In Local Courthouse

Laszlo Varga, confessed killer, will go on trial for the murder of Mrs. Billee Rhae Morning of Wells, Monday morning at 10 o'clock in the district court in Elko.

The sensational development in the case recently, in which a Joseph Barabas was said to be held by Michigan authorities, has collapsed according to District Attorney A. L. Puccinelli. He says he has made every investigation possible and has been unable to determine the existence of Barabas, either in Detroit or Flint, Mich.

A man named Joseph Barabas was named by Varga as the one who forced him to participate in the murder of Mrs. Morning, wife of Rev. Richard Morning, Presbyterian minister of Wells. On June 15, Defense Attorney George F. Wright, appointed by the court to defend Varga, received word from the Lutheran Charities of Detroit that a man named Barabas was being held there for deportation to Czechoslovakia.

Pointing out that his means were limited to investigate the possibility that the man named might have been Varga's accomplice, Attorney Wright asked District Attorney Puccinelli to make such a probe. This has been completed to "the best of my ability" said the district attorney today "and I have found no evidence showing that such a man exists there."

It was on the night of March 22, 1948 that Reverend Morning returned from Montello to find his wife brutally murdered and her body trussed to the bed. Their baby boy was found on the bed near the body asleep.

Officers who investigated characterized the murder as the "most brutal in the history of Elko county."

Varga slipped through the clutches of the law here and a
(Continued on page 6)

150 Elko County Residents Called For Varga Jury

One hundred and fifty residents of Elko county have been summoned to this city for the opening of the Laszlo Varga murder trial Monday morning. From this group will be selected the 12-man jury that will hear the case.

Only one of the 150 persons summoned has failed to answer the summons, but there is still some thought that he will answer before the time of the trial.

Those making up the panel from which the jury will be chosen are: Elko—Jose Aneabe, Ernest R. Barigar, Mrs. Ethel G. Blohm, R. L. Boggan, H. L. Bruce, J. Leslie Carter, G. E. Chapin, Newton H. Crumley, Edith Dean, A. J. Dewar, Burnell Doyle, John Eacret, Pete Elia, Norman H. Feasel, Mrs. Ala B. Fernald.

Fred Fernald, Ruthe G. Gallagher, Jess Goicoechea, Earl R. Green, Jasper Gregory, Tom Griswold, L. P. Harriman, John J. Hunter, Robert L. Kane, Harry Lipparelli, E. L. Littlefield, Oliver P. McCuistion.

Mrs. Pearl McElroy, George F. Ogilvie, Ira S. Pearce, A. M. Peterson, Roy D. Roseberry, Mrs. Sylvia Smith, Guy H. Vega, Eugene F. Wines.

Wells—Robert J. Agee, Jow Mrs. Esther Boies, G.

Parade Winners Announced Today By John Gammick

Lucky Ones Named After Close Contest

Winners in the great parade staged yesterday to herald the opening of the Silver State Stampede have been determined, parade Chairman John Gammick announced this morning.

It was only with great difficulty that parade judges could come to decisions in the several categories in which competition was held. Balloting to determine winners was close, and numerous honorable mentions were listed by the judges, who included Archie Dewar, Howard Doyle, Ralph Smith, Blaine Austin and Jim Dickey.

Following is a list of winners:
1. Best riding club entry, Elko Riding Club.
2. Best mounted ranch unit (2 or more), Moffat Buckaroos.
3. Best merchant entry, Crumley hotels.
4. Best horse-drawn vehicle (2 or more horses), Arthur Glaser of Halleck.
5. Best single horse-drawn ve-
(Continued on Page 5)

No Disorder Says Elko Police Chief

Although the town was packed with people taking part in the first annual Silver State Stampede celebration, the conduct of the crowd was a sight to behold, said the Elko police chief.

"For a large gathering, such as was in town last night, there were no major disturbances, no disorders of any kind. As a matter of fact, it was one of the most orderly crowds I have ever seen," declared Chief Percy Lanouette.

In commenting on the stampede as a whole, the police chief had nothing but praise for the sightseers and townspeople. The

67

the top of the page. This long-awaited rodeo was bringing in the world's finest riders and cowboys to take part in steer wrestling, calf roping, and bareback riding. Add to that the toughest Brahma bulls in five western states and you had yourself the best Stampede ever!

Excitement was running high in anticipation of the day's program at the fairgrounds that Friday, and the place was packed. A crowd of over three thousand was on hand to witness the sights and sounds of the spectacle that was promised. They were not disappointed. From the moment Uncle Bing called out "let 'er buck" into the microphone after opening ceremonies until the end of all the competitions, the people were on their feet cheering.

Bing, Dixie, and the boys were in box seats with Johnny Eacret and his wife, Doris. Being in his "dress" cowboy outfit, Bing was wearing his hand-tooled leather boots with his name on them, further proof of what a special time this was. They all hated to see it end.

The event had been advertised all over Nevada and surrounding states. Knowing that the rodeo would draw a huge crowd to Elko, businesses took out large ads, even in the Green Streak section. The Stockman's Hotel called it "The Biggest Show Ever!" and "In The Round-Up Room To Entertain You Each Evening: The Rocky Mountain Play Boys." Other notices read: "Come One, Come All to the Silver State Stampede. Remember, For a Grand Time, visit the Club Tropic." It seems that the whole town did have a grand time.

It appeared that this event was one of Uncle Bing's first official duties, and it stimulated a great deal of interest and publicity for Elko. When the festivities were over, Bing and his family headed for the ranch. The four boys were out of school for the summer now, so they were able to stay for another month at least.

Shown left to right are Lee Frankovich, Mayor Dave Dotta, Honorary Mayor Bing Crosby, and Dick Warren celebrating "Blue Serge Day" on June 30, 1951.

THESE YOU GOTTA SEE

Bing Leading Parade at Nevada Stampede; Ava Gard
and Bob Taylor Getting Wet Down; Liz Taylor as a Blonde, Allyson as a Brune

BRONCO BING

RIDING at the head of the parade which marked the opening of the Silver State Stampede in
Nevada, is the honorary mayor of Elko, the Old Groaner in person. And looking every inc[h]
rancher in beat-up felt hat, flowing tie, and chaps. The Paramount star (his next film is Conne[cticut]
Yankee) recently bought a 3,000-acre ranch near Elko—his second—and spent most of the su[mmer]
there with Dixie and their four kids. With him above is Newton Crumley, local hotel o[wner]

Bing and his friend Newt Crumley were featured in Movie Life.

"LET 'ER BUCK!" shouted Bing, and the rodeo was on, with Bing, Dixie, and the kids among crowd of 3,300 roaring spectators. Note Crosby's high-heeled riding boots with his name tooled on 'em. At rear John Eacret, manager of Bing's ranches, and Mrs. E.

DIXIE and the boys—from left to right, Dennis, Lindsay, and Philip—wore Western togs for the celebration, and only Dixie's poodle refused to enter into the gaiety. Kids have been working on ranch all summer, will make a movie for Disney this fall.

Seen taking in the rodeo are Johnny and Doris Eacret in background and Lindsay, Phil, Bing, and Dixie in front. Notice Bing's boots.

Chapter Four:
Indian Summer

EVERAL OF THE NEVADA RANCHES THAT UNCLE BING HAD PUR-
chased lie north of Elko by quite a few miles. They were located inside
the county lines and referred to as being in the "North Fork area." These
ranches were at the five thousand foot level, which meant that they had
snow on the ground in the winter months, a genuine white Christmas.
Between Bing's North Fork ranch and the Idaho border lies the Duck
Valley Indian Reservation at Owyhee (pronounced O-wa-hee).

The tribe there is a combination of two, the Shoshone and Paiute. The
people are industrious and the reservation very productive, raising cattle,
horses, and hay.

Because of this far north location of his ranch, about one hundred
miles from Elko, my uncle became acquainted with some of the tribal
members at Owyhee. They were good neighbors, and as such, would help
each other in rounding-up cattle, mending fences, or whatever was needed. Uncle Bing found that these Indian folks had an easy-going manner
about them, much like his own; maybe that's why they got along so well.
He liked the fact that they smiled a lot and had a warm handshake that
spoke of trust. Bing felt at home with these native people; they seemed
to have similar values, and were just down right friendly. Best of all, they
knew who Bing Crosby was, but never made a fuss over him.

Bing was invited to attend their Fourth of July festivities in 1948. After accepting the invitation, he also donated $250 in prize money for the
cow-cutting contest at the rodeo. He became a fairly regular visitor to the
reservation, meeting more and more of the people and taking great interest in their activities and general welfare, especially their access to water

and the Wild Horse Reservoir. After a time, it was evident that Uncle Bing was very fond of this band of Indian people and was impressed by the many educational programs they offered to their children. Also, the tribe was highly motivated and was virtually self-sufficient. These were qualities that I know Bing admired.

It was not surprising that when the tribe needed something, and Bing heard about it, he was there to help in whatever way he could. The hospital fund received a donation from him, as did the Boy Scouts. A fellow named Ralph was an administrator at the hospital during that time, as well as being the tribal clerk. Uncle Bing was broadcasting the *Philco Radio Hour* every week in those days and when Ralph mentioned to him that the scouts wanted to listen to the show, but had no radio, Bing ordered a Philco console with a brass plaque on the front to be sent to the boys. Ralph also visited Uncle Bing's North Fork ranch many times for a variety of reasons. One day he was going there on hospital business and one of the nurses begged to go along. At first Ralph said "no," but she finally convinced him, and they set off for Bing's place. The nurse met Bing, and after Ralph finished his business, the young nurse produced a camera and asked Bing if she could take his picture. Being out of the public eye at the moment, and just relaxing at the ranch, Bing was not wearing his toupee and seemed a bit perturbed at the request. He looked over at Ralph, who was caught completely off-guard and looked embarrassed. Then he turned to the nurse and said, "Okay, but make it snappy sister, I don't have all day." I guess this was the last place my uncle expected to meet one of his fans, and an Indian girl at that.

Ralph came to the Duck Valley reservation in a somewhat unusual way. He belonged to the Sioux tribe and liked living in South Dakota, but couldn't find work there. Then he heard about a job in Nevada. On the phone, the prospective employer said the opening was for a "tribal clerk at Owyhee," but because of Ralph's hearing difficulty, he thought the man said. "Travel clerk at Hawaii."

"I'll take it," yelled Ralph into the phone. Boy was he surprised when he got there.

Certain times of the year Uncle Bing needed extra ranch hands and would hire young men from the tribe for cattle branding round-ups and working with starting colts.

As time went on, Uncle Bing and the Shoshone-Paiute tribe developed a bond of trust and respect to the point that they took him into their confidence and planned ways to honor him.

During the years 1936 to 1938, a dam was constructed on the Owyhee River and became known as the Wild Horse Dam. The land for the dam was purchased by the U. S. Government and held in trust for the Indian tribes on the reservation. As a result of the dam, a reservoir or lake was formed, providing badly needed water for their irrigation system. The lake, approximately three miles long and one mile wide, had never been given a name. However, in July of 1950 during a Tribal Business Council meeting, a resolution was proposed to designate the reservoir as "Bing Crosby Lake." It was then resolved by the council that a letter be submitted to the Secretary of the Interior petitioning for the name to be adopted.

The minutes of the meeting read as follows: "Whereas Mr. Bing Crosby is our neighbor, friend and benefactor, in that he has contributed to our Shoshone-Paiute rodeo and Fourth of July celebrations and has donated money for our hospital at Owyhee and has shown personal interest in our welfare."

The idea of renaming the reservoir was presented to Uncle Bing for his approval when he attended the rodeo and Fourth of July celebration held at the reservation in 1950.

Tribal records show that for reasons previously noted, Bing was also to be adopted into the Shoshone-Paiute tribes, an honorary position. As the first white man in the history of the Duck Valley tribes to be so inducted, and the highest honor ever bestowed on a non-Indian by them, Bing was quite naturally, overwhelmed. He made the statement that he was "thrilled and flattered" at the prospect of becoming a part of the Shoshone-Paiute tribe. "I have traveled around the world," he said, "and along the way I've been given many titles and honors, but this one means more to me than any of the others."

Above: Bing is inducted into the Shoshone-Paiute tribe.
Below: Bing with a baby in a cradleboard.

Above: "Man of Many Songs."
Right: "Regular guy," Bing
with his Indian fans at
Owyhee.

This was a very emotional statement, and we have to wonder why Uncle Bing felt so strongly about it. Was it because these people were Native Americans? Or did he feel unworthy of the honor for some reason? No one has the answer.

Regardless, on Tuesday afternoon, July 25, 1950, famed singer and film star Bing Crosby was given an Indian name and inducted into the northern Nevada tribe.

The ceremony was planned as a simple affair because the Indian people looked upon Bing as a "regular guy." No fringed deerskin outfits or beaded headbands; just everyday clothes. Photos taken at the time show Bing in his usual cowboy hat, worn tilted to the left, the way he liked it, and a western-cut summer shirt, complete with his ever present pipe, visible in the right-hand pocket.

The event attracted a large audience of tribal members to witness the unique event that day. Nothing like this had ever happened before, and the people were curious, especially the elders. Bing and tribal officials were seated on a platform, which also held a speaker's podium, microphone, and Indian blanket. The chairman of the tribal council, Gus Garity, was in charge of the proceedings. After some opening remarks, Garity handed Bing a parchment scroll which read in part, "Mr. Crosby has shown a deep and sincere interest in the welfare of our tribes, and we feel in our hearts that he should be invited to become an honorary member." At that point, Bing was standing next to the chairman and when Garity presented him with a traditional Indian headdress, Uncle Bing removed his cowboy hat and put it on, much to the satisfaction of the crowd. Bing was also given some beaded accessories to complement his new position in the tribe. In return, Bing gifted Garity with a pair of handmade deerskin gloves, made from the hide of a buck Bing shot near his ranch. Although he was there without any of his family, Bing was embracing a new family and new name that the tribe had given him. The English translation of which was: "Man of Many Songs." In keeping with his new moniker, Bing took the microphone and sang a chorus of "Home on the Range," followed by a short rendition of "Blue of the Night" for his new brothers and sisters. Following the ceremony, everyone adjourned to take part in a watermelon feed in celebration.

Although the relationship Uncle Bing had developed at Owyhee was truly outstanding, it was not the first time he was recognized by Indian people. In 1948, the Squamish tribe in Vancouver, Canada, made Bing an honorary member, and gave him the Indian name, "Chief Thunder Voice," along with the typical headdress worn by an Indian chief at that time. The feathered bonnet was displayed in his home at Hayden Lake, Idaho for many years.

Uncle Bing was enjoying some major popularity at the time, as a top recording artist, as No. 1 at the box office, and his radio shows beat out all the competition. Even though his career was going at breakneck speed, he typically found time to help a worthy cause. One of those was the Sunset Community Centre in Vancouver, Canada, a proposed youth center that was sorely needed. For two years the fundraising efforts of their association brought in only $20,000, and then they decided it was time to speed things up. The man in charge of the project was Stan Thomas and it was he who took on the job of scheduling a major event to raise money. The committee felt that mega star Bing Crosby was the right man to help them reach their goal of building the Sunset Centre. The plan was to ask Bing to stage a one-night benefit show. Not only did Bing agree to appear and sing, but also to have the show broadcast over the ABC radio network.

Bing and his troupe of twenty-one traveled from Los Angeles to Vancouver by train, which took forty eight hours. Performing in the show with him were actor Ray Milland and singer Marilyn Maxwell; Bing also brought along his own musicians and technicians to ensure a smooth-running performance. It was a sizeable undertaking, yet Bing was anxious to help promote any number of projects that would benefit youth. Referred to as "that great American," it was reported that Bing refused any payment for the show or cost of transportation. When the performance took place on September 22, 1948, in the Vancouver Forum, the record-breaking crowd of nine thousand added almost $26,000 to the coffers in one fell swoop.

While he was in town, Bing took part in a ground-breaking of sorts when he visited the site of the proposed center. Climbing up into the driver's seat of a Caterpillar bulldozer, Bing took the controls and maneuvered the big beast just long enough to disturb some of the earth. It was a beginning.

Above: "Chief Thunder Voice."
Below: Bing honored by the Squamish Tribe.

Left to right, Bill Morrow, Bing, unidentified friend, and Johnny Eacret display their catch of the day.

Chapter Five:
My Heart Is a Hobo

IN THE LAST WEEK OF MAY, 1951, UNCLE BING WENT ON A FISHING trip in Canada with his radio writer and friend, Bill Morrow. Having caught their limits, (or so they said), the dead-tired anglers packed up and headed back home to Los Angeles. It had been a successful trip, plenty of good times and camaraderie. Being able to enjoy the company of a good friend with a sport he loved was one of Bing's ultimate pleasures. Both the men had been "roughing it" for several days, and while they took care of the necessities of life, even in the wild, they didn't bother to shave or worry about keeping their clothes clean. After all, a serious fisherman didn't take along a tuxedo or fancy clothes, not where they were going.

Because of the driving distance involved, Bing and Bill had decided to stop in Vancouver, British Columbia and stay overnight, even though they had not made any advance hotel reservations. When they found the Vancouver Hotel, conveniently located off the highway, Bing pulled in, parked the car, and they went inside.

It was after dark by this time and Uncle Bing was getting pretty tired and hungry; the thought of a hot shower, decent bed, and real food were the only things on his mind. The hotel clerk appeared from behind the registration desk, and not knowing it was Bing, asked him what he wanted.

"Fix me up with a couple of singles with baths," he said.

The Vancouver Hotel was the swankiest lodging in town, and when the clerk took a look at this fellow in cowboy boots, jeans, and a beat-up leather jacket, he was definitely not the type of clientele that was allowed to come in, let alone rent a room. Because Bing and his pal were similarly dressed and unshaven, the clerk told them there were no rooms available. Giving them both an icy stare, he ended the conversation by adding — "the hotel is booked solid, for days."

As the pair turned to leave, one of the hotel bellhops suddenly recognized Bing. The situation was then made right by the manager who escorted the unkempt duo to their suites on the seventh floor, with a lovely view. Afterward, the clerk was questioned about it, and he said, "It was all a mistake; I thought they were just a couple of bums."

Having now received the royal treatment from the hotel staff, the two fishermen laughed about the mistaken identity and quickly cleaned themselves up before dinner. After consuming a meal fit for a couple of hard-working lumberjacks, Bing and Bill settled down for a night of at least eight hours sleep.

While they snoring, the news media were having a field day with the story of the movie star who almost got "the bum's rush" from a four-star hotel. By the time the two famous guests appeared in the hotel dining room for breakfast the following morning, everyone in town was talking about it, and the rest of the world was reading about it with their morning cup of coffee. The city offices called Bing with apologies and the committee of the Sunset Memorial Youth Community Center contacted Bing, asking him to address their group.

On that same day, Bing paid a visit to the local youth center which he had helped build in 1948. This time he spoke to a large crowd — over one thousand boys and girls. His audience was aware of the incident at the hotel because it had been so well publicized, and he took the opportunity to joke about it, "I'm sorry I didn't bring a shirt with me that would knock your eyes out," he told them.

As he checked out of the hotel later, he said "the next time I come to Vancouver I'll wear my blue serge suit." This particular remark was considered a bit sarcastic because in those days, a dark blue suit was the socially accepted attire for a man to wear to a wedding or funeral. This was one step below formal wear, so to say.

The press had splashed the story all over the country and readers found it hilarious. To think that Bing Crosby, a very wealthy man and world celebrity would be mistaken for a bum and denied a hotel room was quite a laughing matter indeed. Shortly after the story broke, two of Bing's friends in Elko, Newt Crumley and Al Manhan, who were on the committee for an up-coming rodeo, decided that even though Bing was an "honorary" mayor, he needed to be appropriately attired. Knowing that Bing would get a big kick out of it, they carried the "bum" episode even further. Al and Newt must have felt like a couple of kids when they contacted the American Hotel Association and the Levi Strauss Company in San Francisco to place an order for two tuxedos to be made out of their trademark blue denim jeans material. One tuxedo was for Bing and the other for Mayor Dave Dotta. Sewn inside each jacket was a leather label with a message that read:

Notice to hotel men everywhere
This label entitles the wearer to be duly received and registered with
cordial hospitality at any time and under any conditions.
Presented to Bing Crosby
Elko Blue Serge Day, Silver State Stampede
June 30, 1951
Signed: American Hotel Association
By: D.J. O'Brien, Pres.

Mayor Dotta's tuxedo had his own name on the label.

The suits were double breasted with a total of six buttons on the front and four on each sleeve. The jackets were lined in a gray colored fabric, thereby allowing the over-sized lapels to be of the same color when the collars were folded back. Levi Strauss was delighted to make the tuxedos and be part of the spoof; the company even went so far as to create boutonnières made from their red Levi pocket tags. A red handkerchief completed the classic look.

The outfits were shipped to Al Manhan's store. Mostly a men's clothing shop, Manhan's also featured western wear for women and children. Al had the Levi distributorship in town, so it made sense to let him handle everything. Crumley agreed.

The plan was to present Bing and Mayor Dotta with the tuxedos at a special occasion; after all, it wasn't every day that a man received a custom-made tuxedo, especially one that matched his blue jeans. The timing was perfect. The biggest rodeo event of all, The Silver State Stampede, was going to be held on June 30, 1951. Of course Bing would be there, and the publicity was bound to be a big boost to Elko. Thankfully, the tuxedos arrived in plenty of time.

Blue Serge Day

The rodeo started on Friday and went on for three days. Most people bought their tickets ahead of time and were in the stands on "day one" to hear the announcements and to look over the stock and the riders. But this time, the second day of the event was considered the highlight of the fourth annual Silver State Stampede. Declared "Blue Serge Day," by the rodeo committee (in reference to the Vancouver Hotel episode), Bing, along with Mayor Dotta, was going to be presented with his denim tuxedo. The Saturday crowd of two thousand was considered to be the biggest in the history of the four-year event.

The audience was restless with anticipation. At the time, the Stampede did not have the ever-popular rodeo clowns on the program, so

Expanded Bing Crosby display in the theater setting at the Northeastern Museum.

Elko Daily Free Press

Largest Circulation of any Newspaper Published in Eastern Nevada—Published Every Afternoon Except Sunday

ELKO, ELKO COUNTY, NEVADA, SATURDAY, JUNE 30, 1951 — SIX PAGES

World Awaits Cease Fire In Korea

★ ★ ★   ★ ★ ★   ★ ★ ★   ★ ★ ★   ★ ★ ★   ★ ★ ★
Elko's "Mayor" Bing Crosby Given Suit At Stampede

More Trouble Der Bingle Hotel Clerks

Crowd Sees Presentation 2nd Day of Rodeo

Situation Termed Critical As Floods Rage In Midwest

Thailand Troops, Air Force Beat Back Navy Rebels

Fighting Flares As Revolution Set In Motion

UN Stations Air Peace Offer; S. Koreans List Peace Demands

Danish Hospital Ship Is Readied For Peace Talks

7 Contestants To Vie For Title Of "Miss Nevada"

Iowa Resident Succumbs Today At Elko Hospital

Iran Warned It Must Face 'Consequences'

Truman Faces Task Of Signing

LEVI'S TUXEDO

NOTICE TO HOTEL MEN EVERYWHERE. THIS LABEL ENTITLES THE WEARER TO BE DULY RECEIVED AND REGISTERED WITH CORDIAL HOSPITALITY AT ANY TIME AND UNDER ANY CONDITIONS.

PRESENTED TO

BING CROSBY

ELKO SILVER STATE DAY, SILVER STATE STAMPEDE
JUNE 30, 1951
SIGNED AMERICAN HOTEL ASSOCIATION
BY D. J. O'Brien, Pres.

The famous denim tuxedos.

85

it was Bing and the Mayor who would provide the comic relief. Word around town was that Blue Serge Day was not to be missed, which resulted in even the box seats being sold out at the rodeo grounds.

A couple of weeks prior to the event, some of the fellows on the committee got together and built a wooden platform on wheels, which was to be used for the tuxedo presentation and was referred to as "the float."

Rodeo fans and local citizens alike had all eyes on the speakers' stand, waiting for the announcement and introduction. On it was a standing microphone and a tall wooden box affair with a hand-painted sign reading: "Bing's Room." This was provided in order for Crosby and Dotta to change into their new suits in privacy. After donning their denim duds, the pair emerged and showed off for the crowd. Bing held his arms up and slowly turned as if he were a model parading on the runway. Being the acting mayor, Dotta was more conservative in his behavior.

As the two men stood on the platform posing for cameras, wearing big smiles, and enjoying the wild applause, Bing was conjuring up a little ditty to sing to the crowd. Using the melody from "On Top of Old Smokey," Bing sang his own words:

"Way up in Elko,
They know what to wear.
The next time I come here,
I'll have to bring my hair!"

At that point, he removed his cowboy hat, showing that he was quite bald. The audience loved it all, even though it was definitely a break with tradition.

The Stampede was the oldest rodeo in Nevada, having started in 1913, and had hosted prestigious competitions for cowboys ever since. Having become a large part of the Elko community and their activities by now, Uncle Bing had been prompted to get involved in the Stampede. His reputation was that of a man who gives as well as receives, and after the denim fashion show, Bing announced that he had commissioned a tall silver trophy to be made and engraved each year with the winner in the best all-around cowboy category. Uncle Bing's donation was termed a "revolving" trophy, and the practice was continued until 1958. The first year, Buck Rutherford took home the trophy. The following year, a pub-

The denim tuxedo is a perfect fit. Note the flying Levis over Bing's dressing room. Below: Bing exhibits his modeling skills.

lished photo of Bing presenting the 1952 winner, Dell Haverty, with the trophy caught the eye of artist Led McCarty and in 1958 he created an oil painting of Bing from the photograph to mark the occasion.

The rodeo crowd of the Silver State Stampede that year got more than their money's worth; it was a full program of entertainment plus a handsome trophy added to the purse. The stadium seats were filled. Locals as well as folks from Idaho and Utah would never forget what a special day this turned out to be, and it gave Nevada a high ranking in the category of small rodeos.

Bing thought his new outfit was pretty snazzy by all accounts at the time, and he continued to wear it on special promotional days around town. At the conclusion of all the presentations, the float was removed and the cowboys went to work. The first competition of that day was bareback riding.

The atmosphere was in high gear that weekend in 1951, not only with the excitement of the rodeo, but also with the hope of a cease fire announcement, and an end to the Korean War.

Cowboy Dell Haverty accepts Bing's donated silver trophy after winning at the Silver State Stampede.

Above: Bing was seldom without his pipe. Left: Bing and Mayor Dotta pose in their new outfits from Levi Strauss.

Bing Crosby and Jane Wyman turn a wedding march into a riotous race and prove that even in his private life, a newspaperman will stop at nothing to scoop the other fellow

"here comes the groom"

■ Bing's new movie is full of laughs and fun and music —just what movie-goers have been waiting for.

Jane Wyman sings along with Bing. And Bing dances along with Jane.

When director Frank Capra hired two famous wrestlers to coach Jane and Alexis Smith in the not un-gentle art of wrestling, the girls collected plenty of laughs— and plenty of bruises.

The fabulous voice of Anna Maria Alberghetti, thirteen-year-old Italian soprano, is heard for the first time on the screen in this wonderful Paris-to-Boston merry-go-round.

Chapter Six:
In the Cool, Cool, Cool of the Evening

UNCLE BING SPENT ABOUT ABOUT FIFTEEN YEARS IN NEVADA, OFF and on, enough to qualify him as a registered voter of Elko County. By 1951 he had become such a common figure around town that some folks flat forgot that he was there. Yet when a few blockbuster events came along, the people proudly supported him as if he were a native son.

Bing had dominated the front page of the *Elko Daily Free Press* newspaper on at least three occasions: becoming honorary mayor, opening the Silver State Stampede (after a thirteen-year hiatus) and the presentation of the Levi Strauss denim tuxedo at the Stampede in June 1951. However, the granddaddy of them all was when Bing brought Hollywood to Elko.

He was working on a new film, *Here Comes the Groom*, which normally would have premiered in New York, but Bing convinced Paramount Studios to let it take place in Elko, as a fundraiser for their hospital.

The director for *Here Comes the Groom* was Frank Capra. Although Bing and Capra had been working in the film capital for almost twenty years, they had not made a picture together until 1950, *Riding High*, which, along with *Here Comes the Groom*, were two of Bing's romantic comedies that were directed by Capra. Known as a man who was able to draw out the best performance from an actor, Mr. Capra explored the full range of an actor's ability. The Crosby-Capra pairing proved to be a successful one, undoubtedly due in part to the mutual respect between these two artistic men.

It was Frank Capra who found a discarded song in the Paramount archives, written by Johnny Mercer and Hoagy Carmichael, that lay gathering dust and forgotten. Capra thought the tune would be a good duet for Bing and Jane Wyman. More than just good, it proved to be terrific, and the song "In the Cool, Cool, Cool of the Evening" from the film, *Here Comes the Groom*, received the Academy Award for the best song of 1951.

The premiere date for Bing's film was set for the end of July, and with all the extra activities involved, was scheduled to last for three days. A first-ever movie premiere in this locale of five thousand people required an enormous effort on the part of the townspeople. Elkoans had never before dealt with anything of this importance or magnitude. If they ever doubted Bing's popularity or the scope of his influence, this event would make them true believers. Their honorary mayor was a world-renowned celebrity, and not a bad rancher, either.

Once again a committee was formed to help handle the work load. Every hotel or room available for rent was spoken for, well in advance. Orders were placed by the truckload for food, drink, paper products, and supplies of every kind in preparation for the invasion of visitors. It was round-up time in Elko, but not for cattle; the hunt was on for street decorations, outdoor lights, microphones, and the like. Signs and banners had to be made, publicity scheduled, transportation arranged.

Tickets went on sale two weeks before the premiere event, with prices ranging from $2.50 to $12.50, and were sold at both the Hunter and Rainbow Theaters, and the DuPont Pharmacy. Sales were brisk and even Uncle Bing got in on the act when he showed up at the Commercial Hotel in his denim tuxedo to sell tickets. It was a publicity stunt that the local newspaper caught, showing Bing holding a "six gun" on a couple of his friends as a means of encouragement for them to buy tickets to his world premiere. By Saturday, two days before the show, the tickets were just about gone.

The committee had fifteen thousand windshield stickers made advertising the affair. The Elko Chamber of Commerce, working with Paramount representatives, put together special brochures showcasing the businesses and recreational opportunities in the town and the county.

Above: Barbeque celebration for Here Comes the Groom *premiere.*

Elko Daily Free Press

Largest Circulation of any Newspaper Published in Eastern Nevada—Published Every Afternoon Except Sunday

AR   No. 166   ELKO, ELKO COUNTY, NEVADA TUESDAY, JULY 17, 1951   SIX PAG

WEATHER FOREC
Partly cloudy with a ftered thundershowers and Wednesday. Little c temperature, with low to bove 45 and high Wedne bout 95.

emiere Of Crosby Film Set For Elk

e-Fire Agreement Near

tice

Ex-Convict Sought For Part In Colo. Prison Escape Try

CANON CITY, Colo., July 17th (UP)—An ex-convict who touched off an attempted prison break when he hurled a revolver over the walls of the Colorado state prison was sought today in a statewide police search.

Warden Roy Best refused to identify the ex-convict. But he said that questioning of five trustys who took part in the attempted break indicated the gun was thrown over the prison walls to a convict waiting inside.

The attempted break came yesterday when the five trustys, armed with the .38 caliber revolver, ordered guard John Sheesley to open the cells of 11 inmates who took part in a break plot two months ago.

Sheesley refused. In the resulting melee, guard Capt. Chet Yeo, and guard Amon Murley, 50, were wounded when they attempted to aid Sheesley. Yeo was in critical condition.

More Than 100 Firemen To Be Here For Meet

More than 100 firemen from

Hundreds Of Red Troops Surround Truce Talks City

Kaesong Area Is Beehive Of Activity

8th ARMY HEADQUARTERS, Korea, July 17 (UP)—Hundreds of communist troops moved a round Red defenses below the neutralized truce city of Kaesong today on both sides of the armistice highway that UN convoys travel daily.

There was no official analysis of the meaning of the busy Red movements around Kaesong, which followed the 8th army announcement that at least 27 new communist divisions have been rushed to the Korean front to raise Red frontline strength to possibly 720,000 men.

THREE PLATOONS and one company of communists were kept under close watch as they shifted around Red defense posts southeast and south of Kaesong. A 10-mile circle centered on Kaesong is immune to UN attack during the cease-fire talks. No restrictions apply to the Redheld zone south and southeast of the city, the last communist holding in south Korea, but UN pa-

US Seeks To Beat Down Ideas On Missing Diplomat

WASHINGTON, July 17 (UP)—The state department sought today to knock down any ideas that a missing British diplomat knows how many atomic bombs the United States has or the process of making them.

The diplomat is Donald S. MacLean, 38. He and Guy F. DeMn Burgess, 40 disappeared from their British foreign office jobs on May 26 in another notable British breach of security.

The state department concedes, however that MacLean amassed a considerable amount of information on this governments atomic energy program. He got this information in 1947 and 1948 when he was secretary of the combined policy committee which decided atomic matters for the United States, Canada and Britain.

The state department's explanation of MacLean's role in atomic affairs of the three nations was prompted last night by a copyright article in the magazine U. S. News & World Report.

The magazine claimed MacLean "knew how many atomic bombs the west had, what were the uranium resources and how many bombs could be made with existing sources and materials."

The department pointed out that MacLean assumed his job as secretary of the policy committee

DROOP-ALONG AT WORK — Bing Crosby makes sure that tickets are sold to the world premiere of his latest Paramount picture, "Here Comes the Groom" to be held in Elko, July 30. Lee Frankovich, general chairman and Newt Crumley, center, are being given the "treatment" for tickets. All proceeds go to the Elko county hospital building fund.

President Truman Flies To Kansas To Inspect Flood

KANSAS CITY, Mo., July 17 (UP)—President Truman flew here today to inspect flood-strick areas of Missouri and Kansas and a five-day-old fire that flared anew today.

Truman planned to fly over the $750,000,000 flood ravaged area

Behncke Voted Out As AFL Airline Pilots Union Head

CHICAGO, July 17 (UP)—David L. Behncke, founder and president of the AFL Airline Pilots association for the last 20 years, was voted out of office today by the union's board of directors.

The action climaxed a bitter feud between Behncke and board members who charged him with "dictatorial" tactics.

Behncke could not be reached immediately for comment. But in

All Proceeds To Into Building Fund For County Hosp

The eyes and ears of the United States will b on Elko when the world premiere of Paramount "Here Comes the Groom," starring Elko's honored Bing Crosby will be held. It will be the first tim history that a world premiere has been held her

Arrangements for the premiere were announc by Mayor Dave Dotta and Judge Taylor Wines, of the Elko Chamber of Commerce, following with officials of Paramount Pictures Corp.

With the announcement of the world prem ing here also came news that all proceeds from the affair have been earmarked for a million doll lar hospital for Elko county.

Handling local arrangements for the premiere will be Lee Frankovich who has been named general chairman of the Chamber of Commerce's premiere committee. Immediately upon being notified of his appointment, Frankovich pledged his wholehearted support to make the event the greatest in the history of the county.

AT THE SAME time, he called on all the citizens of the county to go all out to aid in making the premiere presentation an outstanding success. Backing up Frankovich's request were the Elko county commissioners who issued a proclamation calling for cooperate in anyway possible.

Said the commissioners "through the effort and generosity of our fellow citizen Bing Crosby, an

World Prem Tickets Pla On Sale To

The Elko Count Building Fund com the "Groom Prem mittee" have place sale for the gala miere of "Here Groom." The pe benefit the Elko pital Building Fun for the evening both Hunter and tres.

Tickets are on and Commercial, and Post Pharmacy show of town and

There was going to be extensive news coverage across the country, including a coast-to-coast radio broadcast. It ended up being one of the most widely publicized events in the history of Nevada. It was so big, in fact, that the local paper printed a Premiere Edition, with no other news on the front page except articles regarding *Here Comes the Groom*. The title of the film was even printed in large bold letters above the name of the paper itself. Now that's **big**! It was as if President Truman were coming to Elko.

Reporters and dignitaries began arriving on Sunday night, when a chartered plane from New Orleans landed at the municipal airport. Thanks to the monstrous publicity campaign, there was a welcoming crowd of around three thousand, the likes of which this cattle town had never seen before. According to the police chief, cars were parked ten-deep around the airport; it looked like the entire town was there. And it was a good thing, too, because a plane that arrived later was a DC-4 from New York carrying at least fifty correspondents. The following is a partial list of the news sources that sent reporters to Elko for the Premiere:

Boston Globe · United Press International · CBS (LA) *Washington News · Detroit Free Press · Monterey Peninsula Herald · Los Angeles Mirror · Pittsburgh Post · New York Journal-American ·* King Features *· Denver Post · Boston American Boston Traveler · Boston Post · Newsreel · Hollywood Reporter Milwaukee Sentinel · San Francisco Chronicle · Omaha World-Herald · Memphis Press ·* WGM New York *· Box Office · Atlanta Constitution · Minneapolis Tribune · Chicago Sun-Times Portland Oregonian · Chicago News · St. Louis Globe Democrat Tex & Jinx · Portland Journal · Cleveland Plain Dealer ·* Hearst Photo Editor *· Salt Lake Tribune · Rocky Mountain News Philadelphia News · Christian Science Monitor · Buffalo News Dallas News · Memphis Commercial Appeal · Indianapolis Star Detroit News*

When the reporters checked into their hotels and went to their rooms, it looked as though someone had moved in already. Placed on the bed was a typical Bing Crosby shirt, a straw hat, a pair of Levi jeans, and

94

Film star Dorothy Lamour joins her friend, Bing, in entertaining the crowd during premiere weekend.

a genuine silver dollar. This was hospitality, Elko style. And if something didn't fit, they just took it over to Manhan's store and Al fixed them up with the correct size. Al had plenty of jeans on hand because the premiere committee had requested local folks to dress in western wear, saying that there should be a "sea of blue denim," especially later at the barbeque. Levi Strauss took care of that idea, sending 175 pair of their best blue jeans — complimentary — for this very special occasion. Understandably, the focus was on Uncle Bing, yet running a close second was his co-star from the popular *Road* pictures, Dorothy Lamour. Usually seen wearing some kind of native garb in her films, the sultry actress looked stunning nonetheless in her western costume with boots and cowboy hat for her Elko appearance. It was noted that she enjoyed a game of chance and would draw a crowd when playing blackjack at the tables. Miss Lamour not only charmed the crowds, but also the premiere committee, who voted her "Official Greeter" for the three-day event. Indeed, she was so popular that during her time in Elko she was given the title of honorary governor of Nevada for forty-eight hours!

Bing in his denim tuxedo, showing his friends the label with his name.

The People Of Elko County

WELCOME

Bing Crosby – The Entire Cast   Producer Frank Capra – Members of
the Paramount Pictures, Inc., Production Staff and Visiting Newsmen
and Radiomen From All Sections of The Nation . . . .

For the Premiere Showing of

Alicia Smith   Bing Crosby   Jane Wyman

"HERE COMES THE GROOM"

Thanks For Your Wonderful Cooperation -- In Making

Possible The Initial "Purse" From Which Elko County

Will Build A New General Hospital

And to our "Honorary Mayor" Bing Crosby: "Bing, the People Of Elko County Think

You Are Tops. Thanks for Your Many Courtesies – And May You Have Continued

Success."

★ ★ ★   ★ ★ ★   ★ ★ ★

idcast Event Tuesday Night

Reno Newsman Says 'Old West' Lives In Elko

Bennyhoff Gives Impressions Of Big Premiere

By BOB BENNYHOFF

Somebody once said the "Old West" is dead but pardner, he was wrong. Dead. wrong.

He'd never been to Elko and he certainly had never attended the celebration of the world premiere of Bing Crosby's latest picture, "Here Comes the Groom."

It's not exactly the kind of "Old West" that was in the days of blazing guns, Judge Lynch and the Red Eye Saloon.

But to the visitors from way out west and way back east, it's been one heck of a celebration.

TO A VISITING newspaperman, it starts out quick. Everything's waiting for you when you step off the plane—in fact, most of Elko was at the airport. There must have been at least 3,000 people on hand to say "howdy,"

Bing and Jane tie knot in "Here Comes the Groom"

Bing Came--He Saw--He Stayed

Above: Bing with his sons and the two children who appeared in Here Comes the Groom. *Below: Bing prepared for "The Elko Show" on CBS radio. Left to right: Dennis, Lindsay, and Phillip join their dad at the Hunter Theater for the film premier.*

Chapter Six: *In the Cool, Cool, Cool of the Evening*

On the "premiere" night, Bing and three of his boys rode a horse-drawn buggy to the Hunter Theater. Bing was sporting his famous denim tuxedo and a cowboy hat. The area in front of the theater had been roped off to corral the crowd that had arrived two to three hours earlier. A platform was mounted in front of the theater to be used for the street show prior to the movie's debut. The star-studded performance included show business personalities and high ranking politicians. It ran for forty five minutes and was broadcast coast-to-coast by CBS. Simply billed as "The Elko Show," it was said to have reached forty million listeners. Because of radio coverage, ticket sales, and wide publicity, the premiere raised $10,000 for the county hospital building fund. Some donations even came in by mail because Elko had received nationwide attention.

Paramount Pictures held another *Here Comes the Groom* premiere two months later in New York City, but it couldn't compare to the one in this small Nevada town. Bing was their hometown boy who made good and they were so proud of him. The sixty by three-hundred-foot letter "E" on the hillside just outside of town was lit-up every night during the premiere event, as if to replace the searchlight of a Hollywood gala.

Not surprisingly, *Here Comes the Groom* was well-received by the audience and spontaneous applause was heard throughout the showing. Theatergoers declared that "Crosby has a hit on his hands," and "the picture is a dandy;" people exited the theater humming, "In the Cool, Cool, Cool of the Evening." The elected mayor of Elko, Dave Dotta, was reported to have been "thrilled" to have Bing's premiere in his town, and he was quoted as saying the event really "put Elko on the map." It was a unique combination to be sure, an international singing star and world figure, who was also a major movie star, Oscar winner, and radio personality for many years, becoming an integral part of a small hamlet in northern Nevada. What were the chances of that happening? And yet it did. Reports to the committee stated that the premiere gave Elko the jump-start it needed to increase tourism revenue and attract drivers along Interstate 80 to pull off the road and spend some time in their city. All in all, the premiere was a spectacular event that brought gratification to all concerned: the hospital building fund, Uncle Bing, and the town of Elko.

BING CROSBY
& FRIENDS
In Concert

SPECIAL GUEST STARS:
ROSEMARY CLOONEY

KATHRYN • HARRY
MARY FRANCES & NATHANIEL CROSBY
THE JOE BUSHKIN QUARTET
BILLY BYERS & HIS ORCHESTRA
TED ROGERS "THE TOAST OF LONDON"

ONE PERFORMANCE ONLY!
FRIDAY NOV. 26
AT 8 PM

FIRST COME
FIRST SERVED

Tickets now
on sale at the
Aladdin Theatre
Ticket Office

Aladdin Theatre
for the
Performing Arts

ALL SEATS RESERVED
$20 • $15 • $10

Chapter Seven:
Pennies from Heaven

I AM VERY FORTUNATE TO RECEIVE A POSITIVE RESPONSE EVERY TIME I contact the media to talk about Uncle Bing; he is an easy "sell." I have given newspaper and radio interviews in the United States and Canada, plus the BBC in England. While living here in Las Vegas, I got in touch with a nighttime host on station KDWN radio, Pete Moss, who offered me twenty minutes of air time to let me tell his audience some Bing Crosby stories and help promote my book *Me and Uncle Bing*. Pete had a large following of loyal listeners and many of them proved to be Bing fans. They were invited to call in after my interview to ask questions.

A caller by the name of John asked me if I was aware that Uncle Bing had helped to build a church in Las Vegas. When I said "no," he went on to tell me about a one-night concert given by Bing as a fundraiser to build Holy Family Church; the performance took place at the Aladdin Hotel and Casino. This was a big surprise to me; for whatever reason, I had never heard about it. Uncle Bob and his band had performed in Vegas in the '50s, but not Bing. I ran across a news article that helped explain why I was in the dark about the concert: "During the peak years of his career in the 1940s and '50s, singer, actor, and world-class celebrity Bing Crosby was invited to perform in Las Vegas. An offer of one million dollars was made by a hotel-casino at the time for Crosby to appear. Although the amount was very attractive, the singer turned it down. Rumor has it that another proposal was made in the form of a blank check if Bing would do a show on the Las Vegas Strip. Again, it was refused."

As years passed, the whole idea was forgotten and given up as a futile attempt; he was not asked again, that is, not until 1976 when a certain local priest came along with an appeal for his need to have a real church. Knowing that Bing was a Catholic, the priest contacted him and asked if he would come to Las Vegas and croon some tunes for a church fundraiser. When Bing agreed, it was a big news story. However, there was one stipulation to the commitment: Bing insisted that whatever theater was chosen for his performance, it must be easily accessible for the audience. Bing did not want people subjected to a long walk through a big casino. Upon searching every venue in town, the best place that suited his needs was the Aladdin Theatre for the Performing Arts.

So, after appearing with his troupe of entertainers months earlier in England, Bing brought his show to the Aladdin, for one night only, on November 26, 1976.

The Nevada desert can blow a sharp, cold wind in the winter months; don't be fooled by the palm trees and swimming pools. That night in November was just such a time and it was Thanksgiving Day weekend to top it off. As reported in a *Las Vegas Review-Journal* article, Uncle Bing "warmed the hearts of the 6,000 people in attendance." It was also noted that the Aladdin Hotel provided the facilities at no charge. I learned that there was quite a bit more to this story, and in 2006, I sought out the priest who had been in charge of the building project some thirty years ago.

I called and made an appointment to meet Father Benjamin Franzinelli, by now promoted to Monsignor.

As I waited in the visitor's area of the church office, through the window I could see an older man approaching through the office door.

"Hi there," he said, extending his hand. "I'm Father Ben; hope you don't mind that I just came mufti."

"Mufti?" I asked, "Sorry Father, I'm not familiar with that term. What do you mean?"

"I'm in street clothes, without all the fancy get-up."

He was wearing an English style cap, khaki pants, a light summer short sleeved shirt, and white tennis shoes.

"Come this way," he said. "I'll show you around."

Chapter Seven: *Pennies from Heaven*

Something about this man made me think he was of Irish decent rather than Italian. Perhaps it was his roundish face and fair complexion, or the way that his eyes would give a little wink now and then. I pictured him as someone Uncle Bing would take a liking to immediately and cast in *Going My Way, Part Two*.

As we walked toward the interior of the church, Father Ben was a proud tour guide. "The original part of the church is here," he explained, gesturing to a handsome chapel. A woman knelt in prayer on the left side of the room; she did not acknowledge us, because she was so deep in thought.

"How peaceful it is here," I said, "I should come here more often."

"I'd be delighted to meet with you again," said Father Ben. "You know," he continued, "you are the first member of Bing's family to visit my church."

My feelings were mixed. On the one hand I was a bit embarrassed that so many years had passed without any of us paying tribute to his accomplishment. Yet I also felt a certain amount of pride, having the honor of being called "the first."

"I often refer to this as the old church, because it was built in 1977 when the parish was fairly small," the priest went on, "but over the next eighteen years, the congregation grew to such an extent that we had to build a larger edifice."

As we walked through the stillness of the sanctuary, I learned even more regarding this very special church. For example: one of the largest wood beams ever brought into the state of Nevada now graces its ceiling.

"This is the church that Bing built," my priestly tour guide proclaimed. "Its history always has reference to him. Recently I was invited to speak at Notre Dame University and they asked me about it. I was glad to tell them the story. Imagine that, even at Notre Dame."

Father Ben told me that when the stained glass windows for the church were being made, he ordered a special one that would contain certain symbols: pictures that would commemorate the events leading up to his church being built — from saloon to sanctuary — he said.

"Did you say 'saloon,' Father?" I asked.

"Oh yes, that's right, you don't know about the colorful past of this holy place. Getting it started was a real struggle — wait a minute, stop here." A proud smile came over his face — "this is the window I told you about, the one I dedicated to Bing."

The soft, beautiful, pastel colors of the window were now in front of me. It reached from floor to ceiling and was close enough for me to touch it. The scene depicted a woman astride a donkey, holding an infant, with a man leading the animal by a rope. It is known to us from the Bible as "The Flight into Egypt." Around the window were five separate images: the outline of a building labeled "Sundancer," another building marked "Aladdin," a shield (symbol of the Las Vegas Diocese), a store front with a sign that read "1905 — Ed. Von Tobel Lumber Company," and the front view of the completed church.

"The window is in a place of prominence," said Father Ben. "When I'm up on the altar saying Mass and I raise my eyes, the first thing I see is that window. It reminds me of those early days, and the kindness of your Uncle Bing. We never could have made it without him."

He paused, blessed the window, and then made the sign of the cross on himself. We both turned, doing an about face, to enter the new, expanded part of the church. This area was quite large, of modern design, with seating for one thousand of the faithful flock. It was built in 1995.

"Let's go in and sit down," Father Ben said.

He stood aside, allowing me to enter first, while he dipped his finger in the holy water bowl by the door and blessed himself again. As we walked down the center aisle, my guide began pointing out the features of the interior, which included some lovely carved wooden statues of saints, and of course, The Holy Family.

About halfway down the aisle, the priest stopped and indicated the row of benches where he wanted me to sit. We settled into a comfortable spot as this pious man looked around at the vast expansion of the room. "I was just a poor kid from Brooklyn," he began, "when I joined the priesthood. Now here I am years later, building a church, and the founding pastor of Holy Family."

"If you don't mind, Father, let's get to the part about the saloon; I'm dying to hear what happened," I interrupted.

"Oh sure, be glad to," he replied.

We sat there in the church while I interviewed him. Here is what he told me:

"It all started in 1975. The bishop called and asked me to start a new parish in this part of Las Vegas; we hadn't had a new church here in eleven years. I told the bishop that I thought a daycare center was a greater need, but he said no, 'I want a proper sanctuary.' He also told me I would not be given any money to start this project."

As I sat there listening to the eighty-year-old priest telling his tale, I was grateful that he remembered so many details of the experience.

It was Tuesday and the church was quiet, having completed services earlier in the morning. Now and then an elderly woman would arrive to light a votive candle to her favorite saint, but otherwise we sat in hushed respect, the Monsignor and I, as we both brought Uncle Bing back into memory. "I found him to be a gentle person," said the priest, "and whenever I talked to him on the phone he called me 'padre.' It felt good to hear that, very down to earth, just like Bing."

Building a church is a formidable task at best, however to tackle the job without any funds was literally starting to work from the ground-up. Father Ben laid out his plan. The first step was to gather together the people of the area who would comprise his parish. That meant locating a meeting place for very little rent, or better yet, rent free. He needed to find a good Catholic church with an empty hall.

"I started going out into the neighborhoods and meeting people, telling them of the church that was going to be built; 'have chalice, will travel' became my slogan."

The answer to his prayers came one day when a postman who was a member of Father Ben's potential church group told him about a place over on Boulder Highway. "Why don't you go talk to the owner?" asked the postman. "He's a doctor, a cardiologist I think; his name is Russell Miller."

When the priest arrived at the address he was given, he was a bit surprised to see the name of the place — "Sundancer Saloon." Inside, the décor had a country-western theme complete with sawdust on the floor and a well-placed spittoon. As he looked around, Father Ben tried to envision the saloon as a place of worship. It had a bandstand, cocktail tables with chairs, and a large bar which smelled of beer-soaked mahogany. He could, however, see the possibilities and contacted the good doctor. "How much is the rent?" the priest asked. "Not a dime," replied the physician, "but you have to be out before evening on Sundays so we can get ready for business."

Knowing that he had to make this establishment look like a church, Father Ben reached out to the many resources of Las Vegas and the members of his potential new flock. Prior to moving to Nevada, he had been involved with college kids putting on plays back in New York, which gave him the experience of putting stage sets together. He got in touch with some people who loaned him scenery flats from the Edgar Bergen/ Charlie McCarthy show. The MGM Hotel & Casino supplied the plans and manpower. The show business community was eager to help, making it seem like a small-town project at heart. The crew from the hotel got off work at three in the morning and arrived at the saloon to put things together by four o'clock. They were doing this as a favor for the priest and worked quickly because they were anxious to get the job done and go home. The stage hands had everything in place in plenty of time for Father Ben to say Mass on that first Sunday morning.

The transformation from saloon to sanctuary was truly amazing, as it now looked for all the world like a chapel. A couple of the sets even had colored cellophane in the cutouts, giving the appearance of stained glass windows.

Father Ben went on; "when they finished the job it looked really great, the crew was fantastic, we had special lighting and everything, and it looked like a real monastic room. We covered all the nude pictures in the place with tablecloths. The altar I used was a fold-up number, and I had a makeshift confessional next to the john. The saloon was still open at that point on that first morning, and a drunken guy was sitting at the bar. After looking around at the complete redecorating, he asked the bartender if he could use the phone to call his wife. I could hear him say to her, 'get your butt out of bed and get down here, I'm in church already!' That's how real it looked."

Chapter Seven: *Pennies from Heaven*

In July of 1975, Father Ben said his first Mass at eight o'clock Sunday morning and then another one at ten. Some people arrived early to get the lounge chairs, and in all, about two hundred families came. After a time even the bishop celebrated mass with Father Ben; he thought what had been accomplished so far was really great.

Things went along pretty well in the beginning; the congregation was slowly growing and the collection plate with its silver dollars and gaming chips told the priest that he was drawing the working people, including a popular casino pit boss. This lasted for about a year and a half.

Needless to say, I was captivated by the unusual circumstances surrounding the origins of the church. Over an hour had passed since I met this priest and already he had converted me into a rapt listener. I hoped he wasn't getting too tired, or that some religious business need would call him away. But it was soon evident that he had plenty of energy to spare and he was enjoying every minute of our reminiscence.

"What happened next, Father?" I asked, as if this story were some kind of mystery to be solved.

"Well, I'll tell ya," he said. "The Sundancer Saloon was sold and the new owners got rid of the country-western idea and turned it into a topless disco. I was kind of upset about it because I didn't think it would work out. Sure enough, once it changed over, a lot of things were different. During those days, when I would go in to put on my vestments to get ready for Mass, I had to deal with g-strings hanging on top of the sets, and the altar boys were blowing feathers and picking beads off the bar so we could set up and light the candles. So much for life in the theater." He took a deep breath and shook his head, showing his frustration before he continued.

"Now I was facing dire circumstances. I had to move out of the disco and faster toward my goal of having a real church. How to raise some big money — and quick — took over my every waking hour. I figured the best way to get it was to have a celebrity host a fundraiser for me. The two biggest names I could think of were Bing Crosby and Frank Sinatra. So I wrote each of them a letter and asked for their help. Frank sent $5,000 right off the bat. By now it was late August or the first of September. Then I got a call from Bing saying he would do it; 'When did you have in mind for me to come out there, padre?' I asked him for Thanksgiving weekend, knowing that it was probably short notice, but I was getting desperate and figured it didn't hurt to ask!"

"That suits me," Bing said, and they went on to talk about setting the plans in motion for his concert.

"The show was billed as Bing Crosby and Friends, which meant that Rosemary Clooney, Bing's wife, Kathryn, and their children, the Bushkin Quartet, Billy Byers and his Orchestra, and Ted Rogers — a guy from England — were scheduled to perform. The publicity was great. 'Once in a lifetime entertainment event,' the ads said. The tickets were cheap in those days, ten to twenty bucks."

"I hadn't heard from Sinatra yet about making an appearance or doing a concert; nothing was confirmed. I never spoke to him personally on the phone the way I did with Bing; it was always through his attorney or an agent. Anyway, one day Sinatra's people called me and said, 'Frank will come and do a show for you in January; it will be the biggest thing going.' This was great news and I said a prayer of thanks."

The Monsignor paused, looked at his watch and then asked, "Say, are you getting hungry?" It was approaching noon.

"May I take you out to lunch, Father?" I asked. "Do you have a favorite spot where you like to eat?"

"Sure I do," he said. "I'm almost finished with my story, then we can go. Well, when the news broke about Bing going to do a concert in Las Vegas everyone went nuts, because he had never played here before. Once my advisors and committee heard, they forgot all about Sinatra completely and only posted notices in the papers about Bing. They were supposed to put the word out that Frank would be coming in January, but they didn't. When Sinatra's people got wind of the publicity, they were very insulted and Frank's attorney sent me a registered letter that was very caustic. In it he stated that Frank was offended at not being informed about Bing's appearance in November and that he felt he was playing second fiddle to Crosby. So he cancelled his performance promise. We had pre-sold tickets to Sinatra's concert, and by September we had collected 20,000 bucks. We had to return the money. Boy did that hurt. When I told Bing that Sinatra had pulled out, he said, 'Don't worry about it padre; I'll come

108

back and do another show for you'. Thank God, I whispered to myself, because I didn't have enough money yet to finish the job."

Thinking that his problems would be solved and Bing was going to save the day once again, Father Ben continued making plans to start building his church. However, the following year Uncle Bing had an accident and was hospitalized after a fall from the stage in Pasadena, California. All ideas of Bing putting on a second performance were put on "hold" temporarily.

"But this is the very sad part of it all," the priest continued. "The original plan that Sinatra had agreed to called for him to be here and do my benefit on the fourth or fifth of January, I can't remember which, that was in 1977. His mother and her girlfriend were planning to come to Las Vegas for the church fundraiser and then stay over for Sinatra's concert at Caesars the next day. So when Frank cancelled doing a show for me, his mother and her friend rearranged their schedules and changed their plane tickets to travel a day later. That plane crashed, and Mrs. Sinatra was killed."

BING CROSBY
AND **FRIENDS**
AT THE
**ALADDIN
THEATRE**
FOR
PERFORMING ARTS
With Guests:
ROSEMARY CLOONEY
KATHRYN CROSBY
HARRY CROSBY III
MARY FRANCES CROSBY
NATHANIEL CROSBY
The JOE BUSHKIN Quartet
TED RODGERS
The BILLY BYERS Orchestra
Produced and Directed
by WILLIAM LOEB
Staged by BOB SIDNEY

**FRIDAY EVENING
NOVEMBER 26, 1976**

Father Ben paused and lowered his head, as a sign of respect, then went on.

"Of course I had nothing to do with the tragedy, but somehow Frank felt that I did. I understand these things, because I'm Italian myself. I tried to get to him to convey my condolences, but he refused to see me."

"Anyway, Bing came and did the show and after paying expenses, I had enough money for a good start on a church. We finished building with the help of donations and more fundraising, and on October 18, 1978, the church was dedicated. It was a year after Bing died. I sent letters to Kathryn and the kids, inviting them to the dedication, but they weren't able to make it."

"So that's the story from start to finish, from saloon to sanctuary, now, let's go and break bread together."

As we stood and turned to exit the church, I could see what Father Ben had been talking about. Straight ahead was that special window, the Flight Into Egypt, the tribute to Uncle Bing, and Father Ben's way of saying, "Thanks, Bing."

Chapter Eight:
Empty Saddles

AFTER SOME FIFTEEN YEARS OF COMMUTING TO ELKO, IT BECAME apparent that Uncle Bing was losing interest in maintaining his ties to northern Nevada. Now in his early fifties, I suppose he began to take stock of what he had accomplished there, and what might be in the cards for him and his boys in the future. His beloved wife Dixie died in 1952, and the following year he put their Los Angeles home up for sale, but shortly thereafter took it off the market. Published accounts indicate that Bing floundered for a time, then reported back to work with his weekly radio show for General Electric.

Last seen in Elko in the summer of 1952 at the Silver State Stampede with all four of his sons, Bing began traveling more frequently to Palm Springs for a getaway rather than Nevada. A few days here and there dot the calendar of the times he spent at the ranch from 1953–1958. During those years his young sons were growing out of their western wear and into more adult attire. The boys were coming into their twenties by then and finding most of the temptations that our world has to offer, none of which included ranch life in Elko County. A fitting cliché might be — you can take the boys out of Hollywood but you can't take Hollywood out of the boys — the twins and Lindsay took turns performing with their dear old dad on his radio shows. I think at first the boys did it as a favor for their father, but then the more guest spots they got under their belts, the better they liked it and began to think of singing and show business as a future career.

With his sons losing interest in becoming ranchers, Uncle Bing realized that his hope of passing his cattle ranch on to the next generation was gone, and in 1958 he sold everything he owned in Nevada. He kept in touch with some of his close pals for several years, but otherwise, the PX, North Fork, and Owyhee are just memories.

These were the early days of the Crosby brothers trying a show business and singing career. Life *magazine cover, top row left to right: Dennis and Lindsay; Bottom row left to right: Gary and Phillip pictured at a time when their future looked bright.*

Chapter Nine:
Those Were the Days

BEING VOTED HONORARY MAYOR WAS A LIFETIME APPOINTMENT for Uncle Bing, but it did not guarantee him lifetime recognition or popularity in Elko. For the first five years that he was actually involved in the community, appearing at civic functions such as the Silver State Stampede rodeo, Bing was front page news. As he visited northeastern Nevada less and less, his notoriety followed suit. Any mention of him was put on the second page of the Elko newspaper, then on page three, and eventually just some brief note regarding his ranch. At one time he was considered "hot copy;" later he became hardly noteworthy.

For some reason, the Chamber of Commerce, the Tourist Office and the museum have not publicized the story of Bing Crosby in Elko. Nor will you find a "Bing Street," "Crosby Avenue" or any billboard proclaiming "Welcome to Elko — Home of Nevada's First Honorary Mayor — Bing Crosby." It seems odd that the city didn't capitalize on this fame in their history; I've never run across any reference to Bing in any of the information brochures given to out of town visitors.

While I do believe "fame is fleeting" and that Uncle Bing's high-flying days in and around Elko were many years ago, I would think that because he was such a huge presence and influence there, the town would want to keep his memory alive. Perhaps it's a case of "out of sight, out of mind," or that the residents felt he abandoned them when he gave up ranching and sold his properties. Small towns are like that sometimes; they feel betrayed.

In any event, nowadays you would be hard-pressed to find any visible sign of Bing ever having been in Elko, except at their small museum. He is one of those "best kept secrets," almost forgotten.

Some say that Bing was at the height of his career during the ranching years, making more money than ever before. Constantly in demand for films, radio, and recordings, the crooner would leave those Hollywood things behind whenever he could. His heart and mind were in Nevada.

Chapter Ten: *Pass That Peace Pipe*

ONCE I LEARNED OF UNCLE BING'S INVOLVEMENT WITH THE INDIAN tribe at Owyhee, I made plans to visit their reservation.

It was the summer of 2006 when I placed a call to the office of the tribal historian to ask a few questions. The genial voice of Winona Manning put me at ease, especially when she extended an invitation to come and see for myself why my uncle loved to be with the people "up north."

Leaving Las Vegas by way of various highways and state roads heading toward Elko and Owyhee must have been the same route Uncle Bing took after one of his golfing visits. The drive was pleasant and I soon forgot to check the time on my watch. The Nevada desert scenes had a certain relaxing effect all their own and the miles passed quickly, especially along the Great Basin Byway. A number of small towns dotted the map and any one of them were a good bet for a rest stop. I chose the Grade A Café.

Mae had worked the counter at the café for thirty years, so nothing rattled her; she'd seen and heard it all. I liked her right away when she called me "honey" and took my order without writing it down. Mae was a real pro.

The morning I stopped was very busy at the café, as usual, and Mae was going fast and furiously back and forth from one end of the counter to the other. She was wearing a short-sleeve blouse and although her bra strap was hanging down on her arm beneath it, she didn't have time to stop and put it back up on her shoulder. Besides, nobody cared as long as they got their coffee refills.

"You should have roller skates, Mae!" I said as she went racing by.

"I sure could use 'em, honey," she answered on her next trip around, "but not since I got my knee done. Oh, and there's no oatmeal this morning until the truck gets here," she announced.

It was easy to tell that I was in White Pine County; the signs and photos on the walls were a dead giveaway: "Business hours subject to change without notice during hunting season," said one. "Don't even think about asking for credit," said another, obviously geared to local customers. A note on the cooler reminded the workers, "No refills on the good stuff, that means orange juice." Snapshots of hunters posed with their kill were all over the place as well as mounted deer heads with antlers. There was a selection of wildlife paintings by a local artist, along with a sign that read "Prices on all of Irene's paintings are reasonable, or she will trade." Of course the restrooms were marked "Bucks" and "Does."

The Grade A Café was nice and clean, and its loyal customers were well-behaved. All the men ate their meals with their hats on; this was a very casual atmosphere. There was no valet parking.

The lunch "Special" that day was chicken-fried steak with biscuits and gravy, and if that wasn't enough to plug-up your arteries, Mae was sure to suggest topping it off with their famous deep-dish cherry pie and a scoop of vanilla ice cream.

Sitting at the counter was an open invitation for someone to come and sit at the stool next to me and talk my ear off. I really got a feel for the local color. On this occasion, the fellow who planted himself on the empty stool next to me proved to be a bit of a historian.

"The steam engines used to come through here," he informed me. "Yes sir, old '93 and old '40, they only went around forty-five miles an hour, ya know. But I heard tell a number of years ago that they had one engine that could hold the track doing ninety."

By this time I was hoping Uncle Bing had stopped here as well; this was his kind of place, sort of like the DuPont Pharmacy had been.

The charm of the café was enhancing my experience — finding local character. He continued: "I thought about settling in Eureka, a nice little town, a beautiful spot, but they have no medical facilities there and at my age I want that. A visiting nurse would come down from Elko every month or so and set up to see patients in a motel room. But that wasn't enough for me."

When Mae brought our meal, all conversation stopped in favor of eating while the food was still hot. Shortly after that, my lunch date — with his plaid shirt and rainbow colored suspenders — finished what was on his plate and left me to join a friend in the booth behind us. I paid my bill, left Mae a decent tip, and stopped for gas before being on my way again to the north country.

The drive from Elko to the Indian reservation was only about one hundred miles but it took a bit longer than usual, because of the winding roads. As the scenery changed to include more pleasant greenery, I could tell that I was gradually climbing to a higher elevation. Coming into the region known as Duck Valley, with its surrounding hills still showing a hint of winter, it became clear that I was on Indian land. Driving over a cattle guard, a welcoming sign announced the reservation of the Shoshone Paiute tribes. Designed in the shape of a shield, the black and white pattern divides the circle into four parts, depicting the activities that take place here: farming, cattle ranching, hunting, and fishing. Completing the picture are outlines of the states of Nevada and Idaho, as well as a feather on both the left and right side of the shield.

I made my way to Ms. Manning's office in the tribal headquarters and ended up spending several hours with her. An attractive woman and gracious hostess, Winona escorted me to a few of the rooms in the impressive building, stopping to knock on one of the closed office doors. When we were allowed to enter, I found myself facing a room full of men seated at a long table and a female secretary at one end taking notes. Quickly I realized that we had come into a meeting of the Tribal Council! I was well aware of what a special privilege it was, as an outsider, to be permitted entry. Winona introduced me as Bing's niece and asked if any council members had heard of the famous singer and his ties to the tribe. Several men said that they knew the story about the "man of many songs," and some had a father or brother who had worked for Uncle Bing on his ranch. Everyone smiled and shook my hand; it was a warm and memorable experience for me.

Before we left the administration offices, Winona asked a clerk to give me a copy of the tribal documents regarding Uncle Bing. I never would

have been able to get these papers without her help. What a dear lady she is.

Winona suggested that we go over to the senior center for lunch and visit with people there who might have recollections of the old days when Bing came for their Fourth of July festivities. A very few seniors remembered much about him, as it was over fifty years ago, and they would have been small children at the time. After a delicious meal, we went to the home of a woman named Elizabeth who does beautiful beadwork on deerhide. Now a senior citizen, it was she who made the beaded gloves and moccasins

Winona Manning.

Senior Center at Owyhee.

for Uncle Bing when he was inducted into the tribe. I sat in her kitchen and we talked about the time she made the gifts for Bing. She still creates beautiful beaded items and told me that her grandson tans the deer hides for her work.

Then Winona invited me to her home to see some photos of Bing's ceremonial day that she had kept all these years. She had two copies of a magazine article from a 1951 issue of *Movieland*, which contained several photos of Uncle Bing and the people who attended the ritual that made him a member of the tribe. In one of the pictures, Bing was holding Winona's baby sister, Tina, in her cradleboard. I was very thankful when my guide offered me one of the magazine copies to keep as a memento of my visit.

Before heading back to Elko, Winona drove me past the "old" hospital, the one that Uncle Bing had donated funds to help build. Now the windows are boarded-up and the building is no longer used, yet it is far from being in ruins. The tile roof and stone work are still in place and the walls don't even need painting. The chimney made of native rock stands

Tribal member Elizabeth made the beaded gifts given to Bing.

tall and proud over the small, single story building. I have a hunch that this industrious tribe will put the old hospital to good use before too much longer.

I had accomplished what I set out to do there at Owyhee. I suppose this is the part where I should say something like "as we bid a fond farewell to the Indians of Duck Valley," etcetera. Instead of that, I do want to share my heartfelt "thanks" to the warm and gentle people whom I met there, and express my appreciation for their kind hospitality. As a result of my visit, I now have a sense of what attracted my uncle Bing to be a part of their Indian Tribe.

The "old" hospital at Owyhee that Bing helped build through his donation.

Chapter Eleven:
It Ain't
Necessarily So

FOLLOWING THE SPECTACULAR CROSBY-DOTTA DENIM TUXEDO show and rodeo in the summer of 1951, followed by his movie premiere a month later, Uncle Bing does not appear to have returned to Elko much after that. He brought the four boys to the Silver State Stampede one more time, in 1952; Dixie died five months later. It wasn't until May of 1954 that records show him at his ranch again for a few days. Almost a year later, he was back to visit for a couple of days, and then the same pattern continued until 1958 when he sold all of his ranch properties.

In 2004, I learned that a small museum in Elko, Nevada, had Uncle Bing's Levi tuxedo on display in an exhibit, along with the tuxedo once owned by Elko's Mayor Dave Dotta.

Therefore, you can imagine my surprise when I learned that a denim tuxedo, the one supposedly given to Uncle Bing in 1951, was offered for sale in 2006 on eBay, the internet trading post. The asking price was $1,500. The seller didn't mention how he happened to obtain the tux; he only claimed that it was Bing's.

I assume that it was ultimately sold, as most of Bing's memorabilia items have eager buyers. But I suspect whoever did purchase it paid good money for a copy, because the original was said to be on display in Elko.

I placed a call to the museum there and asked if they were selling Bing's tuxedo. "Absolutely not!" they replied, and sent me color photographs to prove their statement. I decided to get in touch with the source of all this, and contacted the Levi Strauss Historical Archives Department in San Francisco. It took a couple of days to search the files, but when the historian returned my call, the information she had for me was like getting a bad report card. Upon examination of the records, she found that twelve to fifteen replicas were made of Uncle Bing's tuxedo, including the leather label with his name on it just inside the front opening of the jacket. I was almost speechless, very confused, and full of questions. How could anyone be sure which denim tuxedo belonged to Uncle Bing, if there was no way to identify it?

I was disappointed to learn that multiple tuxedos were made, thereby spoiling the exclusive one-of-a-kind quality of the piece. On the other hand, who was I to tell Levi Strauss Company how to run their business? I was told by the company representative that the additional tuxedos were sent to their Levi distributors at various stores around the United States. Used as a promotional advertising tool, they were put on display and were to be returned to the company headquarters when the promotion time ended.

One reason I was so interested in pursuing the elusive Levi tuxedo was for authenticity. It was becoming clear with each discovery that every person who owned one of these tuxedos swore it was Bing's, and that it was of great value. I also heard of a store in Tokyo, Japan that claimed to have the original jacket, with an asking price of ten thousand dollars. The situation was getting out of control and looking more and more like the old "shell game." Collectors were in danger of being cheated if they were not forewarned about the copies. I was fascinated before, but now I was determined to do my own investigation toward finding the "real" Bing denim tuxedo of 1951.

My search for the remaining eleven or so knock-offs brought me to a news story in an Arizona paper. In it, a young man was interviewed in 1969 because he said he wore Bing Crosby's denim tuxedo to his high school prom. According to the newspaper article, teenager Gary Greensweig went to a men's clothing store to rent a tuxedo for the school dance. He saw a denim jacket on display and asked the clerk if it was available for rent. The salesman said he thought it would be okay, so Gary paid the rental fee and took it home.

In 2006, I located Mr. Greensweig and spoke to him by phone about his special attire for that evening some fifty-seven years ago. Now an eminent physician with the St. Joseph Health System, Dr. Greensweig said he would be glad to talk to me regarding the experience. As he reminisced about the past, he said that the store in question was called "Lad to Dad." They sold clothing for men and boys and also rented formal wear. The doctor told me that the day he went into the store and saw the denim tux, he knew he wanted to wear it to the dance because he would look so different from all the other boys and he thought it would be fun. He liked the casual look and feel of the jacket, plus, the leather label inside with the name Bing Crosby on it made it even more exceptional. Needless to say, he stood out from all the others at the prom who were wearing the traditional formal wear. Dr. Greensweig confided that the girl who was his date that night was not amused by his choice. He ended our conversation by saying that after he returned the tuxedo to the store, he doesn't know what happened to it.

It was a delightful interview and I thanked him. As busy as this doctor is every day, he even took the time to look for a photo that was taken that prom night and send me a copy. More evidence of what people will do for things concerning Bing. When I received his prom picture, I knew at a glance that it was a replica because of the button hole on the right lapel. Bing's tuxedo never had one there.

At this point I had accounted for three copies of the famous Bing tuxedo, based on the belief that the original was in the Elko museum.

Once again, I turned to the computer in my search to track down more of the reproductions; I was beginning to feel like a detective trying to solve a mystery.

Next I came across a man I'll call Ace Valpone. The story I found on the internet told of this western folk singer who "owned Bing Crosby's denim tuxedo." Using my Sherlock Holmes skills, including a magnifying glass, I found him. His phone number was unlisted, so it was a challenge for me to get in touch with him, but it only served to make me more determined to talk to him. I learned that he lived in a very small town, an area where everyone knows your business and what type of mail you receive. Several long distance phone calls later, my sleuthing techniques paid off. I located a friend of the singer who agreed to take my

Dr. Gary Greensweig attended his high school prom in a Bing tuxedo replica.

125

number and pass it along to Ace; after that it would be up to him if he wanted to speak to me.

About a week later my phone rang, and when I answered it, a voice that sounded like Johnny Cash said, "This is Ace Valpone."

I introduced myself and explained why I wanted to talk to him.

"I understand you have the denim tuxedo once owned by Bing Crosby," I said.

"That's right, little lady," he replied.

"My gosh," I said, "how in the world did you ever get hold of it?"

"Well, I'll tell ya, it was a birthday gift from a friend of mine. He bought it at a garage sale, somewhere in Idaho, I think. Anyway, it fit pretty well at the time and I wore it a few times when I had some gigs on the road. Oh yeah, and I wore it when I went to the Grammy Awards one time. It's in really good shape; I've kept it in a plastic bag, hangin' in the closet. I can't wear it anymore, put on too much weight and can't button it. It really looks best when it's buttoned because it's a double-breasted jacket."

"How can you be sure it really belonged to Bing Crosby?" I asked.

"Because it says so; right inside the jacket is a leather label with his name on it.

"What do you plan to do with it now?"

"Hell, I'd just as soon sell it; you interested?"

"Yes, I might be; what's your price?" I inquired.

"Don't know. Let me ask around and get back to you. Do you know what it's worth? Or, what you are willing to pay?"

"I asked you first," I said, laughingly.

Ace and I left it at that. He agreed to call me in a couple of weeks after he returned from his out-of-town concert.

Now you may be wondering why I didn't tell Ace about the dozen or more imitations that Levi made. Admittedly, I led him on, hoping to find out exactly where it came from, as well as what was the going price for "the real" Bing tuxedo.

He called me two weeks later to say that he had made a mistake; he didn't have the tuxedo in his closet after all. It was being kept at his daughter's house, and she lived in another city. Giving me her phone number and a mailing address, Ace said I should deal with her directly because he traveled frequently and wasn't home very much. I took his advice and contacted Ms. Valpone, who was very friendly at first, but grew cold when I suggested that perhaps the jacket in question was a duplicate. I told her that in any case, I was still interested, depending on the purchase price. She abruptly hung up the phone. Subsequently, I sent her father a copy of the information from Levi Strauss. I never heard from the Valpones again. I suspect they thought I was not telling them the truth and only wanted to get the tuxedo for a bargain price.

So much for copy number four.

Several years prior to all of my investigations, I read in two of the *Northeastern Nevada Historical Society* quarterlies, (Summer 1984, p. 80–81) and (Spring 1988, p.38) that Bing's denim tuxedo was given to Gonzaga University in Spokane, Washington, to be added to their collection of Bing memorabilia that was housed there. When I contacted the Special Collections Librarian at the university, however, she said that they never had any denim tuxedo in their collection.

That very same librarian called me a year later, in 2006, to say, "What a coincidence; someone has just donated Bing's denim tuxedo to Gonzaga." I was stumped! I asked if I might be able to get in touch with that person, and she gladly gave me his phone number.

I wondered if this experience would be similar to the last one I had, if this man would also be disgruntled once I told him that he probably had a replica, not the original Uncle Bing tuxedo, because that was in the museum in Elko.

I donned my Sherlock cap once more and pushed on as this was no time to feel intimidated. I was on the trail of a fifth tuxedo copy, and it proved to be my toughest case.

The gentleman I interviewed told me that he had been connected to the university for several years, but was now retired. Gonzaga is a Catholic college, and the man had become acquainted with the Jesuit priests there. One of the priests had given the man a box of items that he had collected during his years at the school. Forgotten over time, the box lay in the back of a closet until the man conducted a thorough housecleaning after retirement. He dragged the box from the closet and saw that the tape was dry, and the box very dusty. Sorting through the various pieces of treasure that the priest had left to him, the man came to the last item. Rumpled and thrown in the bottom of the box like some sort of a charity donation was a blue denim tuxedo jacket. The priest was now deceased, and the man closed his eyes to concentrate on remembering what the priest had told him about it. "This belonged to Bing Crosby," the holy man had said. "Bing himself gave it to me."

The man insisted to me that the tuxedo he owned was the real thing, the one given to Uncle Bing in time for the Silver State Stampede. When I told the man that I doubted the possibility of the tuxedo in the box being genuine, he became indignant and emotional. He raised his voice to me on the telephone, "*Of course this is the original jacket,*" he bellowed, "*The priest said so!*"

I was afraid to say anything more to the man for fear that he would call me a blasphemer, for doubting the word of a priest. While I have a healthy respect for a man who deals with the almighty, I couldn't for the life of me justify the existence of two genuine articles. "Holy tuxedo," I said to myself, "this quest of mine has brought face to face with someone who swears he possesses Uncle Bing's jacket and has the word of a Catholic priest to back it up!"

Within a couple of months I was at Gonzaga myself. I arranged to meet with the librarian in charge of the Crosby collection, and asked her in advance if I could see the newly acquired "Bing" tuxedo.

The collection of Bing memorabilia at the library is quite extensive and ranges from photo albums, signed documents and autographed publicity shots, to recordings of all sizes of Bing's radio shows, as well as the many familiar songs he recorded, some on gold records (for sales of one million), also a replica of Bing's Oscar. There are so many items, in fact, that the university has maintained a vaulted area on the second floor of the library, a repository containing a multitude of shelves with large boxes. Each piece must be cataloged and preserved. I met with Stephanie Edwards, the librarian, and was escorted into the vault. As we walked through the aisles, she stopped at the last row and took a large white box down from the shelf. Removing the lid and some white tissue paper, she asked if I would like to take the denim tuxedo out and examine it.

128

Chapter Eleven: *It Ain't Necessarily So*

Of course I did and went over it with the proverbial fine-toothed comb. It was badly wrinkled, "crumpled" might serve as a better description. Stephanie had folded it nicely to place it in the box; however, it seemed to me that the garment had not been properly stored or taken care of by the previous owner. I held the jacket up to myself as a measurement for size. Uncle Bing was not a big man, nor was this tuxedo. The distinguishing marks were there: the leather label inside with Bing's name, the brass rivets, and the red boutonniere.

Satisfied with my inspection, but not using the magnifying glass, I thanked Stephanie as we walked over to her office. We talked about the collection for a while and then I told her of my belief that the jacket she had in the vault was a copy of the original, because that one was on display in the Elko museum.

She seemed surprised, but not shocked, and she certainly wasn't angry or upset. Instead, she simply asked me why I had formed that opinion. I recounted to her the facts given to me by the Levi Strauss historian, who subsequently informed me that there is no possible way to identify Bing's original tuxedo from the copies. Furthermore, of the promotional duplicates that were returned to the company's corporate offices, several eventually went missing due to theft. Levi now only has three denim tuxedos in their historical collection. Also, I told her about my own tuxedo experiences so far, with Ace Valpone, the tux on eBay, the doctor who wore it to the prom, this man from Gonzaga, and the one in Japan, all who had no doubts regarding the authenticity of the jacket they owned.

With these five, plus the three at Levi Strauss, I had accounted for eight of the tuxedo copies. Not bad for an amateur detective, I thought, feeling very proud of myself.

The story does not end there, however.

I had the opportunity to personally examine another "original denim tuxedo belonging to Bing Crosby." This one was in that small museum in Elko, Nevada. The first time I saw the "Bing" tuxedo there, it was displayed in a glass case. Then in 2004, with additional memorabilia that was collected, the exhibit was moved to a larger area and expanded, using a theatre stage setting, until 2007. At that time, the entire exhibit was taken down and placed in a storage room, thereby allowing me access to the "Bing" tuxedo for the first time. This was an exciting moment for me, to actually handle the genuine article, the denim tuxedo that Uncle Bing wore in 1951 and that I had read so much about.

The jacket was in excellent condition and also bore the signature leather label inside, on the left. As I carefully looked it over, I noticed that something had been added to the label. Starting in the lower left corner and printed in reddish ink were the words: "Sam Stern B.P.O.E." (Letters identifying the fraternal order of Elks). I did my best to identify this man at the time through research, but without success. Uncle Bing was last seen wearing his tuxedo in some 1951 photos taken in Elko. After that, there was no sign of any denim tuxedo until another one surfaced in 1955 being presented to the newly-elected mayor of Elko, Frank Williams, and later put on loan to the museum. The owner also claimed it to be the original, yet with so many copies still unaccounted for, the altered state of the label, and the disappearance of Bing's tuxedo from view for four years, it did raise some doubt as to its authenticity.

I had been working on the mystery of "Who has the original tuxedo?" for over a year. Being totally perplexed and frustrated is an understatement, but about six months later I got a break in the case. It was during an intense search for information that I discovered a book about Nevada, published in 1969, which stated that Levi Strauss had made a denim tuxedo for Bing, Mayor Dotta, and the Grand Exalted Ruler of the Elks Lodge (B.P.O.E.). The Elks Grand Lodge headquarters in Chicago verified from their records that Sam Stern served as Grand Exalted Ruler in 1952. I learned that Mr. Stern was from Fargo, North Dakota and had served the usual one-year term.

In my opinion, this information, plus other evidence, leaves virtually no doubt in my mind that the "Bing" tuxedo in the museum in Elko is a replica, not the original.

One More Tuxedo

Ever since I learned that over a dozen imitations of Uncle Bing's blue denim tuxedo were made, my curiosity led me to find as many of them as possible. The search took me to the historian of the Levi Strauss Company in San Francisco, who was enormously helpful. She probed the vast

Above: Elko museum display. Below: Denim tuxedo jacket given to Northeastern Nevada Museum showing a leather label on the left, inside.

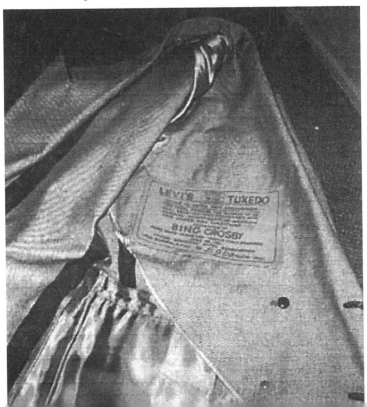

The denim tuxedo shown at the Northeastern Nevada Museum bears this label with the name Sam Stern B.P.O.E. added.

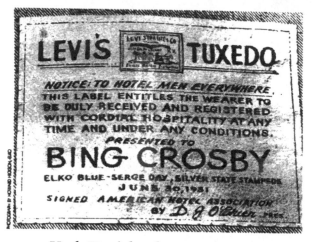

Uncle Bing's hotel room guarantee.

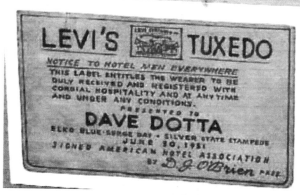

Mayor Dotta's label.

archives of the historic company to find photos and documents, probably braving some spider-filled storage room to go through cardboard boxes of paper receipts from over fifty years ago. I owe her a debt of gratitude.

I was not too surprised then to receive a phone call from the lady at Levi. She told me that she received a message from a television viewer who had watched a program on the history of Levi Strauss, and was very interested in seeing a picture of Bing Crosby's denim tuxedo, because he had the original tuxedo hanging in his closet. I was very flattered to learn that the historian referred the gentleman to me saying, "The expert on the topic of that tuxedo is Bing's niece, Carolyn Schneider"! How true; I had been researching it for almost three years, and had located nine or ten of the jacket replicas, although I had not examined all of them.

The man who claimed to have Bing's original tuxedo was Rex Allen Jr., son of the well-known cowboy singing star of the early '50s. The best part of all this, right out of the "small world" department, is that Rex lived in Las Vegas, not far from our home. Of course, I called him and asked to see his "Bing" tuxedo. He was kind enough to get together with me for a meeting and brought along the denim tuxedo in question.

He said his father told him a story about being in Elko the day Bing was presented with the specially made tuxedo by Levi Strauss. Rex thought that Bing later gave the tux to his father, and then Rex Jr. inherited it when his father passed away in 1999. Upon examination, I had to tell him that in my opinion, the jacket was one of the copies. He accepted my evaluation very graciously, and went on to say that he had similar experiences. It seems that from time to time people came forward claiming that they owned his father's pistols.

Rex had a few more stories to share about his dad, including one that had him on a plane with Uncle Bing flying from New York to Los Angeles.

Rex Allen Jr. sings country-western songs and is also the main force behind his father's museum in Allen's home town of Wilcox, Arizona. Rex plans to display the "Bing" tuxedo there, as it also has his dad's name on the inside label, printed on the lower left.

As of this writing, the original Bing tuxedo still eludes me. However, on a positive note, by working with the Levi Strauss historian, we have discovered ways to actually identify the "true" denim tux worn by Uncle Bing, when it comes to light. Although some records indicated that the replicas were "identical" to Bing's, our further research found subtle nuances of difference after all.

Copies or replicas are a good thing, I believe, if they are used as a visual reminder of something we choose to remember.

However, I also think they deserve to be declared as such and not falsified. When we see the copies of my uncle's Academy Award Oscar statuette, for example, it brings back memories for us of Father O'Malley and life in the 1940s.

Rex Allen Jr. shows me his Bing look-alike denim tuxedo.

Chapter Twelve:
Y'all Come

AMONG A MYRIAD OF PUBLISHED ARTICLES, THE ONE EVENT IN ELKO that Uncle Bing was responsible for, and which has never been equaled, was the premiere of his film, *Here Comes the Groom*. Because of Bing's long and successful show business career, Paramount Studios allowed him to premiere the movie in Elko before it was shown in New York. As a result of Bing's star power and general broad appeal, the movie fundraiser was a huge success.

After the three-day party was over, people still talked about Mayor Dotta's quote to the media, that Bing's premiere had "put Elko on the map."

Many years later, in 2004, the small Bing Crosby display at the Elko museum was expanded to include newly-acquired memorabilia and an oil painting of him with his horse. Colorful record album covers and movie posters, vintage Christmas cards and photographs helped to create an interesting and well-rounded tribute to the famous singer and actor.

However, all that changed three years later. The exhibit was taken down and returned to its original small glass case in the museum.

Gone is virtually everything that related to Bing's stunning career; only a small poster from *Here Comes the Groom* remains. The rest of the items and photos now are of cowboys and ranches, totally ignoring the man's music and voice, films, Academy Award, and long-running radio program. Show business reminders are no longer allowed in the display, although it was Bing's universal celebrity status that prompted Elko to embrace him, and cast their votes to make him the first honorary mayor in Nevada.

According to news reports in the *Free Press* and others, Bing Crosby was a celebrity rancher who figured very prominently in the history of Elko. Bing is the sole subject of the *Northeastern Nevada Historical Societies Quarterly* publication of summer 1984. Bing's influence on the town and Elko County were noted as well in other quarterlies of 1982, 1988, and 2006. Even the Nevada north phone directory of 2004 boasts of Bing Crosby on page thirty. Also the fifty-page booklet entitled, *Elko, Nevada* by Howard Hickson published in 2002 by the Northeastern Nevada Museum and Historical Society contains a nice article about Bing on page thirty-four. Under the heading of Chronological History of Elko in said booklet, Bing Crosby is listed twice on page forty-eight, noting him as "famous singer and actor."

For a man who put Elko on the map, there is no printed evidence of Bing on a map, or anyplace else for that matter.

Without a doubt, Uncle Bing so loved his ranches and life related to Elko that he often invited friends from California to "come up and stay a while." On those occasions, even the ranch hands took a break from routine to play tour guide on horseback, escorting guests to "the back forty" on a pack trip. He brought many people to Elko over the years, and he probably would continue to do so if he were still here. As he said in this song, "Y'all come and see me now and then."

Above: The old museum display. Right: The "new" Bing Crosby display in the Northeastern Nevada Museum. The only reference to his entertainment career is one news report of the **Here Comes the Groom** *premiere.*

BING CROSBY

ELKO'S HONORARY MAYOR

137

Chapter Thirteen:
We'll Rest at the End of the Trail

FATHER BEN'S CONGREGATION WAS STILL MEETING IN THE SUN-
dancer Saloon on Sundays when Uncle Bing passed away in October,
1977. The concert of the previous year had given the priest his start-up
money, but Bing had left some unfinished business. Ultimately, additional funds were collected to furnish the church without him. It was
said at the time that many Las Vegans remembered him fondly, but none
were more emotionally affected by Bing's death than Father Ben. His
makeshift church at the Sundancer with its fake cathedral windows and
candles on the bar, held a memorial service in tribute to their benefactor,
and seven hundred of the faithful attended.

Bing was briefly associated with another church in Las Vegas, when
he married for a second time, to actress Kathryn Grant. St. Anne's was
chosen for the nuptials and the couple spent their wedding night at the
Sands Hotel, courtesy of Bing's old friend, Jack Entratter. Interestingly,
Bing died ten days before their twentieth wedding anniversary.

Definitely not known as a "Vegas guy" the way Sinatra and others
were tagged, Bing nevertheless had formed many friendships in Las Vegas through golfing. Upon his death both the *Review-Journal* and *Las
Vegas Sun* printed front page stories about the life and times of "Der Bingle," although the report could just as well have been covered by *American Angler, Golf Digest,* or *Ducks Unlimited.* Bing was an avid supporter
of those three sports.

Up north in Elko, the media made note of Bing's death and interviewed those who knew him well from the ranching days. It had been

just short of twenty years since Uncle Bing had paid a visit to his old haunt, and several of his pals weren't around anymore. Newt Crumley was killed in an accident in 1962, and others who went hunting or fishing with Bing were not very active anymore. He had kept in touch through the years with a few friends like John Oldham and the Botsfords by phone, letters, and Christmas cards.

Bing's death was worldwide news, but in the accounts of his life and career, very little mention is made of his years in Elko, and his love for the people of Nevada.

Fait Accompli.

Leaving a Legacy

LAS VEGAS THE HOME OF THE CHURCH THAT BING CROSBY HELPED BUILD

Northern Nevada was home to **Bing Crosby**'s seven ranches. His Las Vegas legacy was The Church That Bing Built.

Responding to a priest's desperate plea, Crosby, best known for his 100 million-selling song "White Christmas," agreed to perform at a church fundraiser on the Strip less than a year before he died.

Las Vegas resident **Carolyn Schneider** recounts the story in her second book — currently unpublished — about her famous uncle, the legendary crooner who won an Oscar for "Going My Way" in 1944 and teamed up with Bob Hope in seven "Road to" films.

The concert took place Nov. 26, 1976, at the Aladdin Theater for the Performing Arts.

"Without a proper church and no money to build one, the priest had been saying Mass in the Sundancer Western Saloon on Boulder Highway," she writes in "Bing: On the Road to Elko."

"With the help of the crew from the MGM, scenery was constructed to transform the interior into a chapel on Sunday mornings.

"When the saloon was sold and turned into a topless disco, it was too much for **Father Benjamin Franzinelli**," she wrote.

"The alter boys had to get the (boa) feathers off the bar before they could light the candles," Franzinelli, now a monsignor, told Schneider.

That was the last straw. Franzinelli made an appeal to Crosby, a devout Catholic.

The church that Crosby helped build is Holy Family at Mountain Vista Street and Harmon Avenue. A stained glass window commemorates the history, including a nod to the disco with the risqué reputation.

The window features Mary, Joseph and infant Jesus. In the four corners and one center bottom are five small images: the outline of a building with "Sundancer" on it, the next is the outline of the Aladdin, then a shield (symbol of the Las Vegas Diocese), a storefront image with the date "1905 Ed. Von Tobel" Lumber Co. and lastly is the front view of the completed church.

Crosby died 11 months after his Las Vegas appearance at age 74 after a round of golf in Spain.

Crosby's only daughter, **Mary**, will be appearing with **Desi Arnez Jr.** in the play "Love Letters" on Jan. 24 at Desi's Boulder Theatre. The event is a fundraiser for the Boulder City Ballet Company operated by Desi's wife, **Amy**.

ASSOCIATED PRESS FILE PHOTO
A Nov. 26, 1976, concert by Bing Crosby helped fund the creation of Holy Family Catholic Church at Mountain Vista Street and Harmon Avenue.

Sources

Me and Uncle Bing, Carolyn Schneider, Xilibris Corporation, 2005

Bing — A Diary of a Lifetime, Malcom MacFarlane, International Crosby Circle, 1997

Bing's Friends & Collectors Society

James V. Brown Library, Williamsport, Pennsylvania

Clark County Library District, Las Vegas, Nevada

Crosby Family

Elko Daily Free Press

Elks Grand Lodge, Chicago

Elks Lodge #1152, Hobart, Indiana

Elks Lodge #260, Fargo, North Dakota

Elko, Nevada, Howard Hickson, Northeastern Nevada Museum and Historical Society, 2002

Mrs. Gwen Harvey, Farnborough, England

International Club Crosby

Levi Strauss & Company, San Francisco, California

Nevada's Northeast Frontier, Edna Patterson, Louise A. Ulph, Victor Goodwin, University of Nevada Press, 1991

Nevada magazine

Nevada State Library & Archives, Carson City, Nevada

Northeastern Nevada Historical Society Quarterly

Northeastern Nevada Museum

Personal interviews

Reno Gazette-Journal

Special Collections, Foley Center Library, Gonzaga University, Spokane, Washington